Herbert G. [from old catalog] Winkler

Vegetable forcing

Parts I, II, III

Herbert G. [from old catalog] Winkler

Vegetable forcing
Parts I, II, III

ISBN/EAN: 9783337374792

Printed in Europe, USA, Canada, Australia, Japan

Cover: Foto ©Lupo / pixelio.de

More available books at **www.hansebooks.com**

VEGETABLE FORGING:

PARTS I, II, III.

BY

HERBERT G. WINKLER,
COLUMBUS, OHIO.

THE WINKLER BOOK CONCERN.
1896.

Entered according to Act of Congress in the year 1896,
By HERBERT G. WINKLER,
in the Office of the Librarian of Congress at Washington.

INDEX.

	PAGE
Asparagus	68
Beans	86
Beds	120
Benches	118
Celery	85
Cold Frames	150
Cucumbers	49
Egg Plant	75
Forcing House, Cost of	94
Glass	109
Butted	112
Glazing	111
Strips	113
Hot-Beds	145
Location	145
Uses	146
Construction	147
Preparation for Planting	148
Hot Water Heating	126
Iron Houses	103
Lettuce	5
Proper Temperature	7
Light	8
Soil	9
Transplanting	12-16
Varieties	13
Preparing for Market	17
Peas	88
Radish	61
Rheubarb	64
Steam Heating	132
Sub-Irrigation	136
Tomato	18
The House	20
Sowing the Seed	21
Transplanting	21
Final Arrangement of Plants	22
Trellis and Supports	23
Training and Pruning	24
Pollination	27
Soil and Fertilizers	31
Tomato as a Spring and Early Summer Crop	34
Tomato Diseases	38
Ventilators	115
Water Bench	141

PART I.

MANAGEMENT OF
GREENHOUSE CROPS.

VEGETABLE FORCING.

CHAPTER I.
LETTUCE.

PERHAPS there is no other crop grown in the greenhouse that is so profitable as the growing of lettuce. During the winter and spring months lettuce is always in good demand at very remunerative prices. Hundreds of acres of glass are devoted to the forcing of lettuce in the United States, and the area is continually increasing, although the prices received are far from what they used to be—yet under careful management it can be made quite a paying business.

* "By going back to the early history of lettuce we find that its native country is unknown, and from what species the garden varieties originated is merely guess work. According to Herotodus it was in use 550 B. C., yet Pliny says the ancient Romans knew but one sort. In his day it was cultivated so as to be had at all times of the year, and even blanched it to make it more tender. In the privy purse expenses of Henry the eighth, in 1530, is men-

---
*P. L. Henderson's Hand Book of Plants.

tion of a reward to the gardener of York Place for bringing lettuce and cherries to Hampton Court. Gerard, in 1497, gives an account of eight sorts cultivated in his time. Parkenson, in 1629, says: 'There are so many sorts and so great diversitie of lettuce that I doubt I shall scarce be believed of a great many. For I doe in this chapter reckon up unto you eleven or twelve differing sorts; some of little use, others of more, being more common and vulgar; and some that are of excellent use and service, which are more rare and require more knowledge and care for ordering of them, as also of their time of spending, as some in spring, some in summer and some in winter. For all these sorts I shall need few descriptions, and only show you what kinds doe cabbage and which are loose, which of them are great or small, white, green or red, and which of them bear white seeds, and which of them black.' We have not space to quote the whole chapter, but will quote one more passage: ' Virtues of the lettuce, viz: they all cool a hot and fainting stomach.' "

Lettuce is the most popular of all vegetables grown under glass in this country. It grows rapidly, so that three crops can be taken from a house between September and April, and the demand for a choice product is always good. Lettuce is generally considered to be an easy crop to grow under glass, and yet it is a fact that few gardeners are entirely successful with the crop, year by year, particularly if the heading varieties are grown.

Lettuce varies greatly in quality, and this variation is due in a very great measure to the immediate conditions under which it is grown. If the plant is very rank and has dark thick leaves, the quality is low. A good lettuce plant is yellowish in color upon delivery and the leaves are thin and brittle. The product should be wholly free from lice or green fly, and the tips of the leaves should show no tendency to wither or turn brown. If heading lettuce is grown the leaves should roll inward like cabbage leaves, the heads should be compact and nearly globular and yellowish toward the core.

PROPER TEMPERATURE.

Success in growing lettuce depends very largely on the temperature at which the house is kept. If the house is kept too cool the lettuce will not make as rapid growth as it should in order to be tender and crisp. Lettuce that is grown under a very low temperature, thus retarding its maturity, will be tough and have a strong, bitter taste, and the color will not be attractive. Such lettuce is difficult to sell as there is no demand for it at any price. The temperature should not be too high, as this will induce insects and disease. The night temperature should not rise above 50°, while it may run as low as 40° or even lower. The day temperature in the shade should range from 60° to 75°. At times it may vary somewhat from these figures, but we find that lettuce when grown at the above temperature will give the best results. A sudden change from a high to a low, or low to a high temperature is very injurious. The greatest care should be taken to keep a uniform degree.

LIGHT, SOIL, PLANTING, &c.

While a lettuce house must have an abundance of light, the plants do not suffer if they are some distance from the glass, and if they receive but little direct sunlight. The house should have an exposure toward the sun, and the frame work ought to be as light as possible, if the best results are to be obtained; but diffused light is as good as the direct burning rays of the sun. It should be said, however, that good lettuce may often be grown in heavy, rather dark houses, but more care is required, the results are less certain and there is special difficulty in growing heading varities to perfection.

Our experience has fully demonstrated the superiority of solid earth beds over benches for lettuce. We have had good crops in benches, but they have required special attention to heating and watering, and even then the results are generally precarious. If, however, the benches have no bottom heat—that is, if there is no heating pipes next to them and if the sides are open—very good results, particularly with the non-heading varieties may be had from year to year. When pressed for room the young plants are sometimes pricked off into 3-inch or 4-inch pots, these pots are set in unoccupied spaces amongst the other plants. Very good lettuce can be grown in this way, although it is scarcely practicable in large commercial houses.

Probably no forced vegetable is so much influenced by soil as the lettuce, and no doubt more failures are to be ascribed to uncongenial soil than to any other single cause. Fortunately this matter has been made the subject of the most admirable study by Galloway, who finds that the famous heading lettuce of the Boston gardens can be grown to perfection only in soils which contain much sand and very little clay and silt. The soil allows the water to settle deeply into it and then holds it without percolation; the surface is dry, preventing the occurrence of rot; the roots forage far and wide, and the plant food is quickly available. The full character of the soil used by the Boston growers are set forth as follows by Galloway: "Loose at all times, regardless of treatment, it being possible to push the arm into it to the depth of twenty inches or more. Never puddles when worked, no matter how wet. Clods or lumps never form. A four inch dressing of manure when spaded in ten inches deep will be completely disintegrated in six or eight weeks. Sufficient water may be added the 1st of September when the first crop is started, to carry through two crops and a part of a third without additional applications, except very light ones merely to keep the leaves moist and to induce a movement of the moisture at the bottom of the bed toward the top, where it will come in contact with most of the roots. The surface to the depth of an inch dries out quickly and this has an important bearing on the prevention of wet rot of the lower leaves. The active working roots of the plants are found throughout the entire depth of soil, even if it exceeds thirty inches."

Galloway was able to prepare soil which gave practically the same results as that which he imported from Boston. This soil was made as follows: "Mixture of two parts of drift sand and one part of greenhouse soil. The sand was obtained from the valley of a stream near by, which frequently overflowed its banks, flooding the spot where the material was found. The greenhouse soil was a mixture consisting of one part of the ordinary clay, gneiss soil of the region and two parts of well rotted manure. Such soil will grow twenty bushels of wheat per acre without fertilization."

It is always essential to the best lettuce growing to avoid heavy soils. These soils usually lose their water quickly, necessitating frequent watering which keeps the surface wet and increases danger from damping-off and rot. These soils soon become hard, compact and dead, and the plants grow slowly with thick, tough leaves. If the lettuce crop is to be taken off in the early part of November, from seven to ten weeks should be counted from the sowing of the seed to the delivery of the product. A mid-winter crop may require two to four weeks longer. The time may be shortened ten days to two weeks by the use of the electric arc light hung directly over the house. A single ordinary street lamp of 2000 normal candle power will be sufficient for a house twenty feet or more wide and seventy feet long if it is so hung that the house is uniformly lighted throughout.

The first sowing for house lettuce is usually made about the first of September and the crop should be off in November. We sow the seed in flats or shallow boxes, preferably prick off the plants about four inches apart into other flats when they are two weeks old and transplant them into the beds, from six to ten inches apart, each way, when they are about five weeks from the seed.

Some growers omit the pricking off into other flats simply thinning out the plants where they stand and transferring them from the original flat direct to the permanent bed; but better and quicker results are obtained if the extra handling is given. We have found that it pays to transplant twice before the plants are set in the permanent beds. The first transplanting being made when the plants are only a few days old. When transplanted while the plants are so small they can be set very close together and thus save considerable space.

The second transplanting is made as soon as the plants begin to crowd. If the plants are ready to be set in the permanent bed before the bed is empty, the flats should be placed in a cooler place, or set under the benches for a few days. Plants can be left under the benches for a week, if they are not kept too moist, without any danger.

Four or six weeks after the first seed is sown another sowing is made in flats for the purpose of taking the place of the first crop, and when a third crop is to be grown another sowing should be made four or five weeks after the second sowing.

LETTUCE.

VARIETIES.

Of the vast number of varieties of lettuce there are but few suitable for forcing. The leading ones at present (1896) are the Boston Market or White Seeded Tennis Ball, Simpson and Grand Rapids. About two-thirds of all the lettuce grown under glass is of the above named varieties; but there are numerous other varieties that are grown very successfully. In selecting the varieties the demand of the market should be considered. Some markets demand the headed varieties, while others prefer the loose growing sorts; some are partial to the small heads or clusters, while others demand the largest that can be grown. In some markets there is about an equal demand for all the varieties that are of any account, in fact they don't care anything about the variety, they simply want crisp, tender lettuce. Where the market does not demand any special variety, the quickest healthy growing sorts should be selected. Generally speaking, the kinds that require least bed space are the ones that are most profitable. We will give a brief description of a few of the leading varieties that are most suitable for forcing:

GRAND RAPIDS.

This variety developed at Grand Rapids, Michigan, and is especially adapted to greenhouse culture in winter. It is the result of fifteen years selection from the Black Seeded Simpson, which has generally been recognized as the standard for forcing for house use. It is superior to, and more beautiful in, appearance than the Simpson.

It is of a very rapid, upright growth and may be planted close; not liable to rot; standing several days after being ready to cut without injury; retains its freshness a long time after being cut, hence much sought after by dealers and especially shippers; the quality is very desirable. It does not form a solid head, but the leaves grow in a large loose cluster, hence makes a very beautiful appearance when properly prepared for market.

EARLY CURLED SIMPSON.

This is still the most generally useful variety for all purposes. Properly speaking, it does not head, but forms a close, compact mass of leaves, which are of a yellowish shade of green, and much curled. This peculiarity allows it to mature quicker than varieties that form firm heads. It is the kind that is largely planted in cold frames; it is also largely grown as an early open air variety, between the rows of the cabbage crop.

LETTUCE.

BLACK SEEDED SIMPSON.

Like the Curled Simpson, this variety does not form a head proper, but it differs from the preceding in being much lighter colored, the leaves being creamy yellow; it attains a size nearly double that of the Curled Simpson. It stands the summer heat well, while it is equally suited for forcing. On account of its large size, however, it might not, under some circumstances, prove so profitable as a strictly forcing sort, such as the Grand Rapids, Boston Market, &c.

BLACK SEEDED TENNIS BALL.

A favorite forcing variety, and, as the name indicates, forming a hard head. It makes few outer leaves, and for this reason, can be placed quite close under glass—from six to seven inches apart. This is a very desirable characteristic, as glass covered area is very valuable. This variety is largely used in hot beds and cold frames.

BOSTON MARKET OR WHITE SEEDED TENNIS BALL.

This is an improved variety of the Tennis Ball which attains a larger size. It grows very compact, is beautifully white and crisp, and is one of the best varieties for forcing.

PARIS WHITE COS.

Although the Cos varieties of lettuce are not so suitable for our climate (as they tend too quickly to run to seed) as the varieties previously mentioned, yet they are sometimes grown in the early spring and fall, for private use. In shape, they differ materially from the other varieties, the head being elongated and of conical form, eight or nine inches in height, and five or six inches in diameter. The color of this variety is yellowish green. To be had in perfection, it requires to be tied up, to insure blanching. Millions of this variety are annually grown to supply the markets of London alone, where it is preferred to all other varieties.

TRANSPLANTING TO PERMANENT BEDS.

This is quite an important operation, and most growers pay too little attention to it, that is, they do not realize the importance of using every means to give the plants a good start.

Before taken from the flats, they should be set in the water bench and thoroughly soaked. The plants should be graded into different sizes, so as not to have large and small plants together in the same bed. All the plants in any certain section of a bed, should mature at the same time, so as not to have any vacant spaces.

After the plants have been set, they should receive a thorough watering. If they have been properly transplanted, they will show no signs of wilting, but will start to grow immediately.

LETTUCE.

The plain of setting most generally followed, is to set in squares, but I prefer to set them in the diamond shape. By this plan, the number of plants that can be set on a given space, is increased one half.

PREPARING AND PACKING FOR MARKET.

Lettuce should be cut early in the day, washed and let drain before packing. For our home market, we pack in the ordinary half bushel split basket. The basket is stood on end and the stalks laid in, top end toward the bottom of the basket. When packed in this way, it will retain the moisture and thus keep fresh for a greater length of time than when packed in any other way. When packing to ship, we use barrels or boxes, that will hold about one hundred pounds. If a larger amount is packed together, there is danger of heating.

The barrels or boxes should be well ventilated, by boring holes in the sides and ends. If the lettuce is shipped during the cold winter months, and there is danger of freezing, the boxes should be lined with paper or some other good non-conductor.

CHAPTER II.

TOMATO.*

THE tomato was first introduced into England in 1596, and it was for many years grown only as an ornamental plant, and for its medicinal value. In the earlier days of its history we find the name of Love Apple instead of tomato, applied to this vegetable. In 1629, Parkinson describes the tomato as follows: "In hot countries where they naturely growe, they are much eaten by the people to cool and quench the heat and thirst of their hot stomachs. The apples are also boyled or infused in oyle in the sunne."

Italy was the first country to grow the tomato as a vegetable, and soon after England and France began its cultivation; in England, however, it is chiefly grown under glass, as their summers are not warm enough to ripen the fruit to anything like perfection. The tomato has not been in general use in this country for more than fifty or sixty years, and our choice varieties are of recent introduction. Year by year new varieties obtained by selection from the best varieties are offered to the public, "each one claiming

---
*Henderson's Hand Book of Plants.

to be superior in earliness and productiveness; the varieties of late introduction are undoubtedly superior to the older sorts, earliness, solidity and productiveness being the great desiderata."

The tomato is one of the most important of all garden products; hundreds of acres are now planted with it in the vicinity of all large cities, and the facility with which it is managed places it readily under the control of the least experienced, that is in out-door culture.

During the last few years tomatoes have been grown quite successfully in this country under glass, both as a mid-winter crop and as a spring and early summer crop. The winter forcing of tomatoes promises to be quite an important industry in the near future, although at present it is little understood by most gardeners and the literature on the subject is scarce and unsatisfactory. Yet it is becoming more common year by year, in all the older parts of the country, especially in and around the suburbs of all the larger cities where the winters are cool.

The demand for winter tomatoes is very good and constantly increasing. The price ranges from thirty to eighty cents per pound, according to quality and time of ripening. A high temperature and an abundance of sunshine are essential to force the crop to perfection, but under good management and care in growing the profits are indeed very remunerative. It is one of the most interesting and satisfactory enterprises for the Horticulturist during the dull winter months.

THE HOUSE.

Almost any forcing house that is light, tight and has sufficient pipes to maintain a high temperature throughout the coldest part of the year, is suitable. It should be of a sufficient height to allow proper training of the plants. The frame should be as light as possible and maintain the strength of the house. For further description see chapter on houses.

Tomatoes require the direct sunlight to do well. When the plants are shaded in any way, they will not produce fruit, although they will produce strong, healthy, vigorous growth.

The ill effects of shade are visible upon the north side of benches in houses running east and west, where the plants are shaded somewhat by the center of the house.

During the middle of winter it often happens that the north bench produces no more than half as much fruit as the plants in direct sunlight. The plants in partial shade grow as well and as large as those in full sun, and they often blossom well, but the fruit does not set.

The tomato house should be kept at a temperature ranging from 60° to 65° at night and ten degrees higher on dull days. On bright days it may be allowed to run higher, 90° or even 100° will do no injury, if plenty of ventilation is given. We always begin to ventilate when the thermometer shows 70°.

SOWING THE SEED AND TRANSPLANTING.

If it is desired to have the plants in full bearing during the holidays, the seed should be sown about the 10th of August. The seed boxes should be filled with light, rich soil, pulverized fine; mark off the rows, two inches apart and a quarter of an inch deep; drill the seed rather thick in the rows; smooth over the surface and firm gently with the hand; place the flats in the water bench and irrigate. When they are thoroughly moist, place them over a brisk bottom heat, for tomato seed requires a high temperature to germinate. When the plants are about two inches high, prick off into other flats, setting the plants about two and one half or three inches apart. Leave in flats until they begin to crowd, then transplant into four inch pots, where they remain until planted into permanent beds or boxes.

FINAL ARRANGEMENT OF PLANTS.

This depends much on the arrangement of benches, heating and height of house. We have had excellent success by setting the plants about eighteen inches apart in solid beds as well as in raised benches.

In bulletin 28 of Cornell University, Mr. Bailey says:

"They may be planted in the ground or floor of the house, but I think that this is not desirable as it does not allow of the application of bottom heat and the plants grow slowly; and it is frequently an advantage to shift the plants somewhat during subsequent treatment.

"I prefer to grow them over brisk bottom heat, and it is necessary, therefore, to place them upon benches. The plants may be grown in shallow beds upon the benches, or in boxes or pots. Altogether I prefer 18-inch square boxes, although we have had excellent success in beds.

"The boxes are placed ten inches or one foot apart and four plants are set in each box, which are 18 inches square. A plant, therefore, occupies about one and one-half square feet of floor space. We have grown then in 10-inch square boxes and also in 10-inch pots, but these dry out so quickly that we do not like them. Our boxes are a foot deep; one or two narrow cracks are left in the bottom; a good layer of potshreds or clinkers are placed in the bottom for drainage, and the box is then filled two-thirds full of soil. When the fruit begins to set, the box is nearly filled with rich soil and manure.

The object of not filling the box at first is to confine the roots in a smaller space and therefore hasten fruitfulness—perhaps an imaginary advantage—but more particularly to allow of an additional stimulus to be given the plant at fruiting time."

We think this plan of Mr. Bailey's has some advantage, but we have never tried it in our houses. We always set our plants in the beds and have met with success each year. In our houses they do as well in solid beds where there is no bottom heat, as in raised beds with four strans of one and one-fourth inch steam pipes under them.

TRELLIS AND SUPPORTS.

Different modes of constructing trellis have been adopted. It is not essential which is used, but the cheapest and most substantial is to be preferred. Stakes may be driven by the side of each plant—common lath will answer the purpose very nicely—and they are quite cheap and durable. Another method, used where the house is not too high and the plants are set in beds, is to stretch a wire on the surface of the bed along the rows of plants, binder twine is tied to the wire at each plant and fastened to an eye screw in the sash bar. This trellis has much to recommend it, the plants are not tied to the strings but are simply twined around them, thus saving considerable labor.

When the plants are set in boxes the strings may be fastened to the sides of the boxes in place of having a wire. An excellent plan is to set every forty or fifty feet a strong, substantial post or iron rod, deep into the soil, leaving four feet above ground, at the top of these posts is stretched a wire and at each plant a lath is stuck, the top being tied to the wire. The plants are then tied to lath as often as need be.

TRAINING AND PRUNING.

This is a very important part of the work. Tomatoes under glass *must* be trained and pruned, not only to increase the size and earliness of the fruit, but to get the largest yield possible on the smallest space, and to keep the plants in good shape. It has been found that single stem training will produce the earliest as well as the most fruit per square foot of ground surface. "The nature of the tomato is not to confine itself to a single stem, and when compelled to do so its efforts to grow side branches are very persistent. Not only will sprouts come out at the axil of each leaf, but the ends of the blossom stalks will develop into branches and even the upper surface of the main vein of the leaves will throw out sprouts. All of these must be taken off or there will be a mass of tangled vines if the plants are very close together."

When the plant is twelve or fifteen inches high it should be fastened to its support by means of a soft cord or otherwise; care being taken to remove *all* the side shoots as they make their appearance, and the main stem is stopped or pinched off as soon as it reaches the glass, if not before. In houses of sufficient height the plants may be allowed to grow six or eight feet, if preferred. During the dull, cloudy days of mid-winter it is necessary to remove a portion of the foliage in order to let in plenty of light, this can be done without any injury to the growth of the plant.

The leaves on the lower portion of the plants die when the fruit begins to form and should be removed. I have often seen in our houses, healthy, vigorous plants in full bearing entirely destitute of leaves for two feet from the ground.

After the fruit has set it grows very rapidly and the weight increases to such an extent that the flower stock will break if it is not supported. This can be done by passing a string around a joint on the main stem and under the middle of the cluster.

A row of tomato plants may be planted along the north wall of a house occupied by other plants and trained up the wall. Being thus situated they will not shade the other crops and in a large house quite a number can be grown.

I have heard of growers allowing plants to be trained along the ridge pole and sash bars, but I am sure this would not be profitable as it would shade the other plants in the house to such an extent that they would not mature well.

The tomato does not require so much water as most other plants, that is, during the winter forcing. The soil should not be drenched, yet it should be pretty thoroughly soaked at each watering, and the waterings not repeated so often. When the plants are young and before the fruit begins to set, the atmosphere may be kept moist, especially on bright days when the walks may be sprinkled. A moist atmosphere is detrimental to the Red Spider, and every precaution should be taken to keep the plants free from this pest, for it cannot be overcome after the fruit begins to set; when the house must contain a dry atmosphere. Watering depends somewhat upon the condition of the weather and character of soil used in the beds. No definite rule can be laid down.

POLLINATION.

Mr. Bailey, in Bull. 28 of Cornell University experiment station, says :

"When the flowers begin to appear the atmosphere must be keep dry during the brighter part of the day in order to facilitate pollination. The pollen is discharged most profusely on dry sunny days. In the short dull days of midwinter some artificial aid must be given the flowers to enable them to set. The common practice is to tap the plants sharply several times during the middle of the day with a padded stick. This practice is perhaps better than nothing, although tests which we have made upon the value of this operation as compared with no attention were entirely indifferent in results. I am strongly of the opinion that it will pay the commercial grower to transfer the pollen by hand during mid-winter; at this time the flowers are most likely to fail and the product is most valuable; and the tests which I am about to report concerning the influences of different quantities of pollen strengthen this advice. There are various methods of pollinating the flowers. The most expeditious and satisfactory method which I know is to knock the pollen from the flowers, catching it in a spoon, watch glass or other receptacle and then dipping the stigmas of the same or other flowers into it.

There is a time in the life of the flower when the pollen falls out readily if the air is dry enough to hold dust. This is when the flower is fully expanded and somewhat past its prime. The flower is tapped lightly with a lead pencil and the light yellow powder falls out freely."

"I am glad to give the experience of C. J. Pennock, Kennett Square, Penn., a Cornell graduate, upon this point. Mr. Pennock grows winter tomatoes for market, and he writes me as follows, concerning the pollination of the flowers:

'During the short days of winter I pollinate carefully every day, and I consider the operation necessary. I use a tool of my own make. It is a light piece of wood, 16 inches long and one half inch square, one end of which has a slight saucer-like depression. This stick is held in the left hand with the depression under the blossom to be pollinated. Another light stick or reed is used to tap the blossom and shake out the pollen, the ends of the pistils being pressed into the accumulated pollen in the depression at the same time. On a sunny day, when the house is dry, the operation can be performed rapidly. I have tried jarring the plants, and have seen a brush used, but do not consider either as good as the above method.'

"In the brighter days of March and later, I have found no other attention necessary than keeping the house dry at mid day. But there appears to be further reason why hand pollination is profitable. In my earliest experiences in tomato forcing, I was impressed with the fact that indoor tomatoes are smaller than those grown out of doors, and the midwinter fruits are usually smaller than those produced under the same circumstances in late spring. There is also a marked tendency for house tomatoes to be one-sided. It was a long time before any reason for these facts suggested itself. I finally came to feel that this irregularity and perhaps the smallness, were due to irregular or insufficient pollination, although it is probably true that lack of sunlight has something to do with the inferior size. The first definite aid toward the solution of the problem was the result of an experiment performed early in the winter by my former assistant, W. M. Munson. Mr. Munson pollinated two fruits on the same cluster, with pollen from one source, but in one flower very little pollen was used and it was applied to one side of the stigma only, while the other flower received an abundance of pollen over the whole surface of the stigma.

"The flowers that received an abundance of pollen, produced large and fully developed fruit, while those that received only a small amount, produced small inferior fruit. Moreover, the large fruit was practically symmetrical, while the small one was one-sided.

"The larger fruit had all the seeds developed, while the smaller one had seeds upon one side only, and the other, or unfertilized side, was seedless and nearly solid. This experiment has been repeated several times with substantially the same results. The flowers, of course, were emasculated in the bud, and were securely covered with bags to prevent any interference. Four important lessons are to be drawn from these experiments:

"1. One-sidedness appears to be due to a greater development of seeds on the large side.

"2. This development of seeds is apparently due to the application of the greater part of the pollen to that side.

"3. An abundance of pollen applied over the entire stigmatic surface, by increasing the number of seeds, increases the size of the fruit.

"4. The pollen, either directly or indirectly, probably stimulates the growth of the fruit beyond the mere influence of the number of seeds; the growth of the solid part appears to indicate this.

"The secondary influence of the pollen in increasing the size of fruits, both by increasing the number of seeds—which necessarily demand a larger envelope or recepticle—and by some stimulating influence which it may have upon the pericarp itself, is well known as a scientific fact, but I do not know that it has ever been applied to the practical operations of Horticulture.

"If I have interpreted these experiments correctly, they mean that a part, at least, of the smallness and perhaps all of the one-sidedness of house tomatoes, are due to insufficent pollination, and that it will pay the grower in midwinter to pollinate by hand, and to exercise pains to apply an abundance of pollen over the whole surface of the stigma."

SOIL AND FERTILIZERS.

It is a common belief, that the tomato, unlike most plants, is not benefited by rich soil or heavy fertilizing. It is claimed that the vines make a very luxurient growth, but produce very little fruit. This, however, has been proven erroneous. The fault, I think, lies in the application of too *slow acting* fertilizers.

The plant will outlive any northern season, and its life, therefore, is determined by contingencies of frost, rather than by any inherent limit of duration.

The plant *never* matures in the northern states, and it would probably continue to bear for some months, if not destroyed. Plants have been known to live through two winters in good bearing condition. It is apparent, therefore, that any fertilizer which is not at once available to the plant, but which gives up its materials comparatively late in the season, will maintain a vigorous growth, and probably delay fruitfulness. Coarse stable manures are among this class. It is some time before they become thoroughly decomposed and incorporated with the soil, and if applied heavily, it is probable that they will give unsatisfactory results. If the season were long enough to allow the plant to live out its natural life, it is conceivable that the materials would be gradually used and that the total productiveness of the plant would be as great, if, in fact, not greater, than it would have been, under a treatment which caused it to bear heavily at an earlier period.

In greenhouse cultivation, the great desiderata is to have a full crop produced in a very short time. Therefore, a rich soil containing a large amount of plant food, and quick acting fertilizers, should be used. Of course, heavily manured plants undoubtedly require more care in the pruning, and it is possible, that when not properly handled, they may be more liable to mildew because of the dense and crowded growth; but on the other hand, we always get the best yield from the strongest plants, and we find the extra cost of training to be of very little account.

We select the richest loam we can get, to which is added a fourth of its bulk of well rotted stable manure, and when the plants begin to bear, extra stimulants are added, such as liquid manure, dissolved nitrate of soda, etc. Quite often a top dressing of manure is given. It must be remembered that in house culture, the roots are confined in a small space and they have but little chance to search for food. Hence this heavy manuring is essential to give satisfactory results.

CHAPTER III.

TOMATOES AS A SPRING AND EARLY SUMMER CROP.

THE prices that can be obtained for this crop are quite remunerative. Houses that have been used during the winter, for forcing lettuce, radishes etc., can be used to a very good advantage in growing a tomato crop after the season for winter crops is over, and the space is not needed for anything else. Working with this object in view, we use the houses for other crops while the winter season lasts, and keep the tomato plants in as small a place as possible. which space is not large enough to be seriously missed. As a general rule, houses that have been used for forcing lettuce during the winter and early spring months, are vacant after the middle of May, and produce nothing after the last crops of radishes and lettuce are taken off. Houses can in this way, with almost no cost for fuel and no extra expense for filling benches with soil, be made to produce quite an increase in income, the main work being the growing and and training of the plants.

The demand for these house-grown tomatoes is very good. In the midst of the strawberry and raspberry season, tomatoes sell at fifteen to twenty cents per quart, just about double the prices received for berries. In all markets of any account, tomatoes are shipped in from the South, but do not hurt the sale of those from the greenhouse, being inferior in quality and selling at lower prices.

"In order to get plants ready to set in the beds about the middle of March, or as soon as the last crop of lettuce is cut, the seed should be sown about the middle of December. If the seed is sown much earlier than this, the plants will become too large, and are liable to injury from crowding. No special care is needed in germinating the seed, but the young plants must have good care.

Tomato plants are like corn in that they need all the warmth and sunlight they can get, and at all times they should be kept in the warmer part of the house, and never allowed to get chilled.

The soil should not be allowed to get dry, but excessive watering should be avoided.

After the plants get their second or third leaves they should be transplanted, and at least once more before they are large enough to be put where they stand while fruiting. When transplanted the first time, the plants are set two by two inches apart, and four by four inches the second transplanting. The plants may be set in beds or pots, but for various reasons flats are preferred. When the plants are set where they are to stand for fruiting, they are planted directly in the soil eighteen or twenty inches apart each way. We have used large pots or boxes, but without any apparent advantage, although this custom is recommended for winter forcing.

The last transplanting should be done some time in March, for after the middle of this month the benches can not be used for lettuce profitably, as the houses are liable to get too warm, and the plentiful supply of hot bed and cold frame lettuce, brings the price down ; but when the tomato plants are set out, if good lettuce plants are set between them, a fair crop of lettuce may be grown before the tomato plants reach any considerable size. But after the lettuce is off, the tomatoes should have the entire ground, and should be given a good mulch of fine manure, which will assist in holding the water that is applied to the bed. After the lettuce is off, or before, the tomato plants should be trained to one or two stalks.

VARIETIES.

Nearly all of the varieties that are valuable for out-door culture are suitable for forcing.

Of the purple kinds, the Acme and the Beauty are perhaps the best. Among the red kinds, the

Perfection and Paragon are good. The Lorillard is not so very desirable for forcing, although it has been highly recommended by some. The rough, irregular varieties are not at all desirable.

The Dwarf Champion has some good qualities in its favor. On account of its short compact growth, the plants can be set closer together than any other kind. They can be set in beds that are close to the glass, hence are very suitable for the side benches in low houses.

The first fruit that are set, are of fair size, while on some other varieties they are small, but do not produce very large crops. It has a very dense foliage, and the leaves hide the sprouts, making pruning quite difficult.

Quite a number of other varieties have been forced, but they do not have any special qualities that render them desirable.

At the present time (1896) I know of no better varieties than the Acme, Beauty, Perfection, Paragon and Dwarf Champion.

CHAPTER IV.

SOME TROUBLES OF WINTER TOMATOES.*

NEARLY all forced plants are subject to many diseases and annoyances, arising from the fact that the enemies, as well as the hosts, are protected by the congenial and equable conditions of the glass house. As the cultivation of a given plant becomes more common and widespread, new enemies are likely to find it. The tomato is rapidly becoming an important winter crop, and its enemies are therefore coming into prominence. Two of these troubles—the winter blight and root-gall—are so obscure in their methods that growers often fail to recognize them until the crop is ruined; and as they already appear to be widespread in the north, it has been thought best to call attention to them.

WINTER BLIGHT.

The most serious disease of forced tomatoes which I have yet encountered is what, for lack of a better name, I propose to call the winter blight. This disease, so far as I know, has not been described except in a short communication from this Station in *Garden and Forest*. It has

---

*Bul. 43, Cornell University, Experiment Station.

not yet been carefully studied in the laboratory, but various attempts have been made to check it; and as it is likely to prove a serious disease, the attention of both growers and experimenters should be called to it. The object of the present report is to record the disease and to draw attention to it, rather than to present any full analysis of it. The disease first appeared in our houses in the winter of 1890-91, when about a dozen plants were somewhat affected. At this time the trouble was not regarded as specific; the plants were old and had borne one crop, and it was thought that they were simply worn out. In some of our experiments it became necessary to carry about a dozen plants over the summer, and these were introduced into the house when the forcing season opened last October. From this stock, the trouble again spread and in six or eight weeks it had become serious and there was no longer any doubt that we were contending with a specific disease.

This blight attacks the leaves. The first indication of the trouble is a dwarfing and slight fading of the leaves, and the appearance of more or less ill-defined yellowish spots or splashes. These spots soon become dark or almost black, and the leaf curls and becomes stiff, the edges drawing downward and giving the plant a wilted appearance. The spots grow larger, until they often become an eighth of an inch across, or even more, and they are finally more or less translucent. This injury to the foliage causes the plant to dwindle, and the stems become small and hard. Fruit production is lessened, or if the disease appears before flowers are formed, no fruit whatever may set. In two or three instances, in which young plants were attacked, the disease killed the plant outright, but a diseased plant ordinarily lives throughout the winter, a constant disappointment to its owner, but always inspiring the vain hope that greater age or better care may overcome the difficulty.

It is probable that the disease is bacterial in origin and it was at first thought that it is identical with the bacterial potato blight and that our plants had originally contracted the disease from soil taken from an infested potato field; and this view was supported by the testimony of others who had been troubled with it and who had taken soil from potato plantation.* Specimens were submitted, however, to Dr. T. J. Burrill, of the University of Illinois, who replies that the trouble is probably not the same as the potato disease. A diseased tomato cion was grafted into a potato plant, and the stock for some inches below the union became diseased and

---

* "In Horticulturists' Rule-Book, 2d ed. (p. 59), which was going through the press at this time, the statement is made that "the bacterial potato-blight or rot also attacks tomatoes." I do not know if this statement is true.

finally died; and this potato stock abounded in germs to all appearance like those infesting the cion, but inoculations from pure cultures were not made and it is not safe to say that the tomato disease can be transferred to the potato. Potatoes were planted in boxes containing diseased tomatoes and they did not contract the disease; and a crop of potatoes was also grown on one of the benches in the tomato house, separated from the diseased tomatoes only by a three-foot walk, and it remained healthy. Tomato plants at this distance from affected plants invariably took the disease. It was then thought that the disease might be identical with the southern tomato blight described by Dr. B. D. Halsted in Bulletin 19 of the Mississippi Experiment Station. Specimens were sent him, when it was found that the two are distinct both in external appearance and in the character of the organism, the germ of the southern blight being a bacterium while this is a micrococcus.

All that is known further concerning the probable cause of the disease will appear in the following report from Professor W. R. Dudley, who has made some preliminary examinations of the diseased plants:

"I find a species of micrococcus present in limited numbers in the cells of the tomato leaves, both in those which were blanched, indicating the earlier stages of this disease, and in those blackened by its later development, and also in the diseased fruits. Moreover, the external aspect of this disease—the blackening or blighting of portions of the plants—is such as characterizes diseases occasioned by bacteria in other plants. Nevertheless, the preliminary cultures made did not give any results supporting this theory. Sterilized nutrient agar-agar* was infected with sap from the diseased tomato leaves and fruits with no result whatever; while similar infection from the stem of a potato infested with apparently a bacterial disease,† gave a cloudy-white growth along the track of the infecting wire and on the surface of the agar-agar which microscopical examination showed to be due to a minute micrococcus. Experiments necessary to the determination of this as a specific organism producing this particular tomato disease have not been made. Nor were other nutrient solutions used, which might have been more acceptable food for the micrococcus in a pure culture.

"I cannot feel sure that this disease was caused primarily by bacteria, which were certainly not present in great abundance. From microscopic examination of a considerable num-

---

*Agar-agar is a gelatinous vegetable substance used for making cultures of bacteria.

†This potato stem had been grafted with a diseased tomato cion.

ber of leaves from various sources, and observations in relation to this disease, on winter-grown tomatoes elsewhere, I think that no injurious effects of bacteria will appear, if houses are kept clean, properly heated and ventilated so that the vitality of the plants will not be impaired, and also if the houses renovated at intervals."

Various treatments have been tried upon this disease. Our first attempt was thorough spraying with ammoniacal carbonate of copper, and this is the one which first suggests itself to growers. Our efforts, although carefully made at intervals, were wholly unsuccessful. It was then thought that treatment of the soil in which new plants were set might prove effective, and as our crop was grown in boxes, the experiment was easily tried.

Boxes in which diseased plants had grown were emptied and the insides were thoroughly washed with various substances, as follows: three with dilute solution of ammoniacal carbonate of copper; two with lime whitewash; one with Bordeaux mixture; two with lye. Fresh soil was placed in these boxes and healthy young plants were set in them. The boxes were then placed in the tomato house, near both healthy and diseased plants. For three or four weeks the plants appeared to be healthy, but after that time the disease attacked them all without respect to treatment. The same result followed thorough watering of the soil with ammoniacal carbonate of copper, nitrate of soda, and lye. One box was treated once with ammoniacal carbonate of copper applied to the soil. The plants were somewhat diseased when the treatment was given. The disease progressed without check. One plant died, and a healthy plant was set in its place. This plant was remarkably strong and vigorous for a period of three weeks, when it contracted the disease. In the meantime another plant died from the disease. Late in the winter the remaining plants were removed from the box, the soil was again treated with ammoniacal carbonate of copper and fresh seedlings were set in it; but these plants also contracted the disease. Just before this last treatment was given a 10-inch pot was filled from the soil in the box, and a seedling from the same lot as those placed in the box was planted in it. The pot was set in the tomato house. This plant showed the disease in less than three weeks. The question at once arises if the disease was not communicated through the air from infected plants, rather than through the soil. This I cannot answer, but it is certain that the disease travels from plant to plant which stand in separate boxes, and whose tops do not touch.

Through what distances this transfer can take place I do not know. We observed it to have occurred through a distance of two or three feet, but a plant which stood fifteen feet from diseased plants, but separated from them by a glass partition in which two doors stood open, did not take the blight. It is still possible that we may find a successful treatment for diseased soil, if all affected plants can first be removed from the house.

All our experiments, therefore, simply lead us to the conclusion that the best treatment for this winter blight is to remove all diseased plants at once, and if it becomes serious to remove all the plants and soil in the house and start anew. They emphasize the importance of starting with new plants and fresh soil every fall. And all our experience has shown that the disease is fatal to success in tomato forcing, for we lost our crop in an endeavor to treat it.

COMMON BLIGHT.

(*Cladosporium fulvum.*)—The blight which is oftenest associated with the forcing of tomatoes appears as cinnamon-brown spots on the under surfaces of the leaves. Fortunately, this fungus is rarely serious. For ourselves, we have had no experience with it, but I see it occasionally in tomato houses. It is apt to appear in late winter or early spring, often not until the winter crop is nearly harvested. In such cases, the burning of the old plants as soon as the last fruit is off will be the best treatment. If it appears earlier, however, spraying with ammoniacal carbonate of copper is to be recommended.

ROOT-GALL.

Nematode injuries of roots have received much study of late and the attention of growers has been called to them in bulletins and in the press. But there are still very few horticulturists who are aware of the extent to which they infest our greenhouses. Many common plants, as geraniums, begonias and coleus, are subject to their attacks, and the diseased plant—or the soil in which it grew—is often dumped into the dirt-bin, where it propagates the trouble. In the southern states the nematodes are serious enemies to many plants in the field, even to trees, but in the north they confine their attention mostly to in-door plants. This indicates that severe frost is fatal to them, and suggests a remedy in the freezing of houses which are seriously attacked, when this can be done to advantage, as between the crops of winter tomatoes. Nematodes are very minute animals belonging to the true worms, and allied to the trichinæ. These nematodes are a serious menace to tomato growing under glass. They attack the roots, causing the formation of galls. Sometimes the whole root is swollen into one ragged shapeless mass, strongly reminding one of the club-root of cabbage. The trouble is likely to be worst in those plants which are carried over from the preceding winter. In general appearance, plants injured by root-galls are very like those attacked by the winter blight already described, save that the leaves do not show a spotted discoloration. The plants become weak, stop growing, the leaves curl and become yellow and dry, much as if the plant were suffering for water.

The treatment for this disease is to remove the plants and soil, thoroughly wash the benches or boxes with lye, and begin anew. But it would be a great saving of time and expense if the soil could be treated, between the crops, with some material which would destroy the nematodes. This was tried in a small way. Five boxes, each containing four diseased plants, were selected for treatment December 11th, 1891. The plants were removed, and the soil was treated as follows:

1. One-third pound of concentrated commercial lye dissolved in a pail of water.
2. Two pounds of salt in a pail of water.
3. One pound of quick-lime in a pail of water.
4. Four tablespoonfuls of bisulphide of carbon poured into holes which were quickly closed.

5. The box removed out-of-doors and allowed to freeze solid.

These boxes are 18 inches square and contain 10 inches of soil. Clean young plants were set in them after the lapse of four or five days, and the boxes were set side by side in the tomato house. One or two of the plants died in the soil treated with lye, and the places were refilled, while three settings had to be made in No. 2, because of the great amount of salt in the soil. Between each setting the salt was washed out by heavy watering. When the plants were removed six months afterwards, it was found that all contained galls except those in boxes 2 and 5—those salted and frozen—but upon these no galls whatever could be found. The results were definite and satisfactory, but the experiment was too limited to warrant any general conclusions. They inspire the hope that soils can be treated between the crops for nematodes. L. H. BAILEY.

CHAPTER V.
CUCUMBER.

"THE cucumber is an annual plant, a native of the East Indies, and was first introduced into England in 1573. In the East, the cucumber has been extensively cultivated, from the earliest periods. When the Israelites complained to Moses in the wilderness, comparing their old Egyptian luxuries with the manna upon which they were fed, they exclaimed; 'We remember the fish which we did eat freely, the cucumbers and the melons.' Isaiah, in speaking of the desolation of Judea, says: 'The daughter of Zion is left as a cottage in a vineyard, as a lodge in a garden of cucumbers.'

"In Syria and in India, immense quantities are eaten by the common people. The probabilities are, however, that their cucumbers are melons, though mention is made of the cultivation of both, and late travelers mention large plantations over which constant watch is kept, and fires built at night to keep off the wild dogs and wolves."*

The many varieties under cultivation at the present time are great improvements on the

---
*Henderson's Hand Book of Plants.

original species, but where and when the improvement commenced, we have no record; and it is about as difficult to say when it will stop.

Cucumbers may be forced during the entire winter and spring months. They are also used to succeed the last crops of lettuce and radishes in late spring. If they are to be forced during the fall months, the seed should be sown in the green house about October first, in small pots, three or four seeds in each pot, thinning out to one strong plant. Then in thirty days, or in less time, they will have become sufficiently strong to plant out at twenty to twenty-four inches apart on the south side of the bench.

Some growers go to an old pasture field and cut sod, in pieces two to four inches square. These pieces of sod are inverted on the greenhouse bench, and the seed planted among the fibrous roots of the grass.

When the plants are large enough to transplant, they are taken up and set in the permanent bed. The sod has not yet become decomposed, and a ball of soil will adhere to the roots of the plant. This is quite a good method, but not so practicable as when the pots are used. We use three inch pots, filling them only a third full of soil.

When the plant has formed a pair of true leaves, and stands well above the brim, the pot is filled with soil. This affords additional root space and has the same effect as transplanting.

When the pots are filled with roots, the plants are transferred directly to the beds. Now comes the most difficult time in the forcing of cucumbers. The young plants are very liable to the attacks of insects and fungi, and any failure in the heat will seriously effect them. There are very few vegetables which require such careful attention until they become established. The aphis must be kept off, or the plant will be ruined, even in a few days. A stunted cucumber plant will make a short, bunchy growth at the top, and the leaves will be small and yellowish; it may remain almost stationary for some weeks. Even if it finally resumes vigorous growth, it rarely becomes a profitable plant. Some plants become stunted without apparent cause.

To insure a good stand, it is best to plant three or four times as many plants as are needed, the weaker ones are destroyed, and only the stronger ones are left to bear.

A good plant will grow vigorously from the start and sometimes the lower leaves will fall off, giving it a scraggily and diseased appearance; but so long as the growing parts are vigorous, and the leaves are not attacked with mildew, the plant is in good condition.

The plants should now be trained. Some growers simply place brush on the bed for the vines to run on, but I think this is a poor practice.

The best trellis I know of is made of No. 18 annealed wire. When there is sufficient room above the benches, the plants are trained upon a perpendicular trellis, but on low benches, they are trained along the roof. The wires are attached lengthwise the house in parallel strands from one foot to one foot and a half apart, and cross wires are run down from the rafters every four or five feet to prevent the strands from sagging. The vines are tied upon the wires with raffia or other soft cord. Two or three strong main branches are trained out and only enough side shoots are allowed to grow to cover the trellis, the remaining ones being pinched off as soon as they appear. It is essential that the plants do not become "choked" or over-crowded with young growth, and some of the larger leaves may be taken off in the dark days of midwinter, if the foliage becomes very dense. The branches are all headed in as soon as they reach the top of the trellis or begin to enroach upon the space, allowed for neighboring plants. If the plants grow very rapidly, and the trellis is large, some preliminary heading back may be useful, but we have not practiced the very close pinching in system recommended by English growers.

Growers who find no difficulty in forcing the common cucumbers in winter, often fail with the English sorts. As a rule, these failures come mostly from two errors; insufficient bottom heat, and impatience for quick results. The grower must understand that earliness is not a characteristic of the English cucumbers.

From the sowing of seed to marketable fruits, in mid-winter is on an average from 80 to 100 days. From a month to six weeks is required for the first fruit to attain saleable size after the flower has set. A writer in *"Revue Horticole"* in 1874, records the growing of Telegraph in sixty-five days from the seed, which was the quickest time on record in his vicinity. This was done from February to April, however, when the days are lengthening. The plants continue in bearing for three or four months under good treatment, and a plant ought to yield at least eight good fruits. If the plants are pinched in after the English custom and allowed to bear but two or three fruits at a time, the fruiting season can be extended and probably more profitable, especially in small houses, to secure the returns more quickly, in order to obtain a larger supply at any given time. Care must be taken not to allow the heavy fruits to pull the vines off the support, and those which do not hang free should be held up in slings, for if allowed to lie on the soil they do not color evenly. This swinging also appears to exert some influence upon the shape of the fruit, as will be discussed further on.

POLLINATION.

Cucumbers are monœcious plants; that is, the sexes are found in separate flowers on the same plant. The young cucumber or ovary, can be seen below the petals or leaves of the flower.

The staminate flowers are more numerous than the pistilate, and they begin to appear earlier; a sufficient supply of pollen is therefore insured against all the exigencies of weather or other untoward circumstances. Out of doors the pollen is carried from the staminate to the pistilate flowers by insects, but pollen bearing insects are absent from the greenhouse. If the flowers are fertilized in the house, therefore, the pollen must be carried by hand. There is a question, however, if pollination is advised in the house, for it is certain that the English cucumber will grow to perfection without seed and entirely without the aid of pollen. In the early days of cucumber forcing hand pollination was practiced, but it has been abandoned by many growers. Fertilization was formerly considered necessary for the setting of cucumbers, but it has long been proved to be needless. Indeed, fruits intended for eating are better without, as the seeds in them are not so numerous. For seeding purposes fertilization is decidedly required, if good seed be needed.

Except for seeding purposes it is not necessary that the female flowers should be fertilized, the fruit reaching the same size and being all the better for the absence of seeds. In mid-winter time, or in the care of weak plants, the whole of the male flowers might with advantage be kept removed.

It is possible that the forcing cucumber sets more freely now without pollen than it did before its characters were well fixed, or perhaps the early gardeners performed an unnecessary labor. Many gardeners suppose that pollen causes the fruit to grow large at one end, and therefore try to produce seedless cucumbers for the double purpose of saving labor and of procuring straighter and more shapely fruits. We find, however, that it pays to pollinate by hand if early fruits are desired. The early flowers nearly all fail to set if pollen is withheld, but late flowers upon the same plant may set freely with no pollen. The best way to pollinate is to pick off a staminate flower, strip back the corolla and insert the column of anthers into a pistillate flower.

Fruits which have set without pollination are uniformly seedless throughout, the walls of the ovules remaining loose and empty. Pollination does not occur when the fruits are left to themselves in the forcing-house, especially in midwinter, when pollen-carrying insects are not present.

The production of mis-shapen fruits is one of the difficulties of forcing the English varieties. The commonest deformity is an enlargement of the lower end. English growers often grow the fruit in glass tubes to make them straight. The cause of the deformities, particularly of the swollen end is obscure. The forcing cucumber produces seeds only near the blossom end, the ovules in the remaining half or two-thirds are never filled out, no matter how much pollen is applied to the stigma. It would seem, therefore, that if all these ovules in the blossom end were to develop into good seeds the fruit must be larger at this point; and it would also seem as if accidental application of pollen to one side of the stigma must make the fruit one-sided by developing one cell at the expense of another, for this actually occurs in tomatoes and apples. But it has been found that seed bearing is not necessarily associated with a swollen end of the fruit, and pollination of one side of the flower does not appear to destroy the symmetry of the fruit. It has been found by experimenting with different amounts of pollen, that there is very little difference in external results whether little or much pollen is applied. This is directly contrary to the effect of pollen on the tomato. Little pollen may produce fewer seeds than much pollen, but the shape of the fruit is necessarily influenced; and yet there are instances in which pollination appears to make the fruit unshapely, but why it should exert this influence sometimes and not at others is as yet to be solved. It appears, however, to be a peculiarity of individual plants. It is probable that much of the irregularity in shape is but an expression of plant variation rather than a result of particular treatment.

VARIETIES.

The varieties of the common sorts most generally grown are the White Spine, Nichol's Medium Green and Hill's Forcing.

Of the English varieties, the Sion House is grown most largely for general purposes. It is of medium length, averaging a foot or fourteen inches when fully grown, smooth and regular. It will sell better than the larger sorts in markets which are unaccustomed to the large English varieties.

Telegraph is also a favorite variety, it is a smooth, slender and very handsome fruit, ordinarily attaining a length of eighteen to twenty inches. English authorities say this variety is very liable to mixture.

Kenyon is also an excellent, smooth, slender sort of medium length. Edinburg is a spiny and somewhat furrowed variety, attaining a length of twenty to twenty-four inches. It is not a very attractive variety and many others are to be preferred. Lorne is one of the best of the very large sorts. It sometimes grows as long as thirty-three inches. The very large varieties are less popular than those of medium length. They are too large for convenient table use and they are apt to be inferior in quality to those a foot in length.

The flavor of English cucumbers is somewhat different from that of the common field sorts, the texture being, as a rule, somewhat less breaking. But this is not an evidence of poor quality; it is simply a different quality and evidently belongs to these fruits as a class. The English sorts retain their green color longer than the field varieties. They are ordinarly picked before they attain their complete growth, although they remain eatable for sometime after they have reached maturity.

The reader will now be able to understand what the English mean by " prize cucumbers." Specimen fruits are exhibited at the shows, and there are certain customary scales of points for determining the merits of individual fruits, such as the age, the ratio of thickness to length, the shape of the shoulder or stem end, the color of the tips and the like.

To the student of plant variation, the forcing cucumbers possess unusual interest. As a class, these cucumbers are very distinct from all others, and yet they are known to have come in recent times from the shorter and spiny field sorts, at least those particular varieties which are now grown. It is not improbable that very long cucumbers were known some centuries ago. The *cucumis longus* of Bankin, 1651, is figured, as pointed out by Sturtevant, "as if equaling our longest and best English forms." But these older types do not appear to have been the ancestors of our modern forcing kinds. Our types appear to have originated within the present century. The English have always been obliged because of their climatic limitations to grow cucumbers largely by the aid of artificial heat. We have record, that in 1820, Patrick Flanagan, gardener to Sir Thomas Hare, sent two specimens of cucumbers, one green and the other ripe, to the London Horticultural Society. The green one measured seventeen inches in length, was nearly seven inches in circumference and weighed nearly twenty-six ounces. The ripe one was nearly twenty-five and one-half inches long, eleven inches in circumference and weighed six pounds. Mr. Flanagan states that he has frequently grown these cucumbers in high perfection for the table, nearly two feet long. In 1811 he produced one which measured thirty-one inches in length, was twelve inches in circumference and weighed eleven pounds. This is a remarkable variety of the cucumber, conbining with such extraordinary vigor of growth, so much excellence of flavor as to make it particularly deserving of notice. It keeps true to itself, without variation; but it is difficult to make it yield seed. It requires to be grown in high temperature.

CHAPTER VI.
RADISH AND RHUBARB.
RADISH.

P. L. HENDERSON in his Hand Book of Plants and general Horticulture, says: "The common garden radish is a hardy annual, entirely unknown in its native state. It is usually credited to China. It has long been held in high esteem, and before the christian era a volume was written on this plant alone. The ancient Greeks in offering their obligations to Apollo, presented turnips in lead, beets in silver and radishes in vessels of beaten gold.

"Pliny observes that radishes grow best in saline soils, or when they are watered with salt-water; and hence, he says, the radishes of Egypt are better than any in the world, on account of their being supplied with nitre; modern experience, however, does not allow us to endorse this. He gives some account of the kinds grown at Rome in his day, one of which he describes as being so clear and transparent that one might see through the roots. The radish was introduced into England during the sixteenth century. Four kinds were cultivated by Gerarde in the latter part of the reign of Queen Elizabeth;

since that time many new varieties have been introduced and disseminated by European seedmen and gardeners. The seed is extensively grown in France and Germany, and to those countries we are indebted more for our supply than to any other."

Radishes are one of the chief market garden crops grown under glass. It is estimated that upward of twenty-five acres are grown in greenhouses, hot beds and cold frames near the vicinity of New York.

They are so easily grown that there is no need of giving lengthy directions. The first seed should be sown about the first week in October. When a constant supply is desired successive sowings are made every two or three weeks. From four to six crops are taken from the same ground by the middle of May. The seed is sown thinly in rows three or four inches apart, and the radishes thinned out when an inch high to two inches between the plants. Radishes delight in a rich, rather light sandy soil, well enriched with short stable manure.

When the long varieties are grown, quite a saving of time and space can be had by sowing the seed thickly in flats, and when they are of sufficient size to transplant them into the permanent bed. The oval shaped varieties, however, will not do so well to transplant.

The temperature of a radish house may range from 45°–55° at night and from 60°–75° in the day time.

When large enough for market they are pulled, washed and tied four or five in a bunch, according to the demand of the market, and sold by the dozen bunches. They are usually packed in baskets with the tops down and roots up, giving them a very attractive appearance.

VARIETIES.

Early Scarlet Globe.—One of the earliest and best for forcing; its color is very handsome, flavor mild, crisp and juicy; stands a great amount of heat without becoming pithy.

Early Round Dark Red.—The shape is the same as that of the Early Scarlet Turnip and it differs only in color, and in making much smaller tops. This makes it very desirable for forcing both in cold frames and greenhouses.

Red Forcing Turnip.—The tops of this variety are the smallest of any of the early radishes, which, with its extreme earliness make it especially valuable for strictly forcing purposes.

French Breakfast.—A variety of quick growth, very mild and tender, and one of the best for forcing. Of oval form; color: scarlet tipped with white.

Philadelphia White Box.—Its points of superiority are short top, rapid growth, perfect turnip shape, extra fine quality and showing but little disposition to become pithy, but remaining solid and juicy for sometime after fully grown; especially fitted for growing under glass, in frames or boxes, hence its name. Owing to its very few leaves it can be sown thickly.

Pearl Forcing.—This variety was introduced by W. A. Livingston, of Columbus, Ohio, in the spring of 1891. A most distinguishing characteristic is its rich, waxy appearance. The shape is one long sought for and the most advantageous for bunching, being what might be called half stump rooted. The color is pearl white with the waxy appearance above described, and the texture is very firm and solid. It is about one week later than Wood's Early Frame, but after they are ready for marketing they remain in eatable condition fully two weeks longer before they show any sign of going to seed, and do not become woody. They will not bear quite so close planting as Wood's Early Frame, but their long standing after being ready for market without running to seed, or becoming woody or unfit for table use, more than makes up for the wide planting.

RHUBARB.

Rhubarb has been cultivated from the earliest ages for its medical properties, but was not grown as a vegetable until about sixty or seventy years ago. It was first cultivated in England in 1778. Many varieties have been introduced, for which we are chiefly indebted to the English gardeners. Some of the varieties, under high cultivation, produce enormous leaf-stems; the size, however, is largely at the expense of the quality. Several of the species are very handsome, both in their foliage and inflorescence.

Rhubarb is a plant found in every well appointed garden. It is of the easiest culture, and will grow in sunshine or in partial shade. Of late years rhubarb has been forced quite profitably. It is not unfrequent that when planted under the benches will yield as much profit as the crop on the bench. If forcing is to be continued a good supply of large healthy roots should always be on hand, as the roots after forcing are useless.

In order to have a continuous supply, seed should be sown about the middle of March in a cold frame, in light, fibrous soil, such as leaf mould, so that the young plants will make fibrous roots freely, and thus be easily transplanted. One pound of seed will be enough to sow six 3x6 sashes, and will give about one thousand plants. In four or five weeks after sowing, the plants will be fit for transplanting, which may be done into richly prepared beds of six rows each, at a distance of one foot each way. By fall they will have made fine, well-ripened roots. All that is necessary in the forcing of rhubarb is to take the large roots from the field, which, if well grown, will be from fifteen to twenty inches in diameter, and pack them upright as closely as they can be wedged together (with light soil shaken in to fill the interstices between the roots) under the bench or stage of the greenhouse, or in a warm cellar, or in fact, in any place where there is a growing temperature: say an average of sixty degrees. But little water is needed and none until the rhubarb shows signs of healthy growth. There is no necessity for light; in fact, the stems being blanched by being grown in the dark, are much more tender than when grown in the light and air of the open garden, and are therefore more valuable, besides being forced at a season when they are not to be had in the open ground in the northern states.

Rhubarb is also forwarded in cold frames and hot-beds. When the former is used the roots are taken up in the fall and packed closely together, as is done in forcing houses; they are then covered with leaves thick enough to keep out frost. By March first, the leaves are all removed, except two or three inches, when sashes are put on the frames. By this forwarding process rhubarb may be had from three to four weeks earlier than that grown out of doors.

I have recommended raising the plant from seed, as it is the cheapest and quickest way; and experience has shown that the varieties raised from seeds of either the St. Martins, Victoria or Linnæus come true enough to the originals for all practicable purposes. Those, however, who are particular to have these kinds exactly correct, can obtain them by division.

CHAPTER VII.
ASPARAGUS.

"ASPARAGUS is a native of Great Britain, Russia and Poland. In many other parts of Europe it is found growing wild, but is probably an escape in many localities, and is perfectly naturalized, as it is sparingly on our own coasts. The asparagus is one of the oldest as well as one of the most delicious of our garden vegetables.

It was cultivated in the time of Cato the Elder, 200 B. C.; and Pliny mentions a sort that grew in his time near Ravenna, of which three stalks would weigh a pound. From these accounts it would appear that there is nothing new under the sun in the way of asparagus."[*]

In the forcing house it is treated very much as rhubarb. It will grow under the benches, as it does not require much light. The plants are grown in the open ground on the "surface plan;" that is, they are not transplanted deep in the ground as for permanent beds.

Successive yearly sowings are made so as to have on hand a constant supply of roots. The seed should be sown in the spring as soon as the

---
[*]P. L. Henderson's Hand Book of Plants.

soil will admit of working, which should be prepared by being thoroughly pulverized and enriched with well-rotted stable manure. The seed is sown in rows a foot apart, and if kept carefully hoed and clear from weeds, the plants will be in fine condition for transplanting the succeeding spring. Strict attention to this will save a year in time; for if the seed-bed has been neglected, it will require an extra year for them to attain sufficient size for forcing. In consequence of this very common neglect of proper cultivation of the seed-bed, it is an almost universal impression that plants must be four years old before they are fit for forcing. This is undoubtedly an error, for almost all large growers for market purposes, count on forcing the plants when three years from the seed.

The transplanting may be done any time for six or eight weeks from the opening of spring. The plant, from its peculiar succulent roots is less susceptible from late planting than most other plants, although at the same time delay should not occur, unless unavoidable, as the sooner it is planted after the ground is in working order, the better will be the result. When there is plenty of ground and the crop is to be extensively grown, perhaps the best mode of transplanting is in rows three feet apart, the plants nine inches apart in the rows. In planting, a line is set and a cut made little slanting to the depth of six or eight inches, according to the size of plant. The plants are then laid against the side of the trench at the distance already named, care being taken to properly spread the roots. The crown or top of the plant should be covered about three inches. In a week or so after planting the beds should be touched over slightly with a sharp toothed rake, which will destroy the germinating weeds. The raking had better be continued at intervals of a week or two, until the plants start to grow, when the hoe or hand cultivator may be applied between the rows; the weeds that come up close to the plant must of necessity be pulled out by hand.

GROWING ASPARAGUS FROM SEED

Without transplanting is a method now finding many advocates. It is much cheaper, but requires an extra year to produce roots of sufficient strength for forcing. The plan is very simple and can be done by any one having even a slight knowledge of farm or garden work. Prepare the land by manuring, deep plowing and harrowing, making it as level and smooth as possible for the reception of the seed. Make furrows three feet apart and about two or three inches deep, in which sow the seed by hand or seed drill, as is most convenient. After sowing the seed and before covering, press down the seed firmly in the rows evenly with the feet, then draw the back of a rake lengthwise over the rows, after which roll the whole surface with a garden roller.

In two or three weeks time, if the weather is favorable, the plants will be through the ground sufficiently to define the rows. At once begin to cultivate with hand or horse cultivator, and stir the ground so as to destroy the embryo seeds, breaking the soil in the rows between the plants with the fingers or hand weeder for the same purpose. This must be repeated at intervals of two or three weeks during the summer, as the success of this method is entirely dependent on keeping down the weeds, which, if allowed to grow would soon smother the plants, which, for the first season of their growth are weaker than the weeds. In two or three months from sowing, the asparagus will have attained ten or twelve inches in height. It must now be thinned out so that the plants stand nine inches in the rows. By fall they will be from two to three feet high, strong and vigorous, if the directions for culture have been faithfully followed. When the foliage dies, cut down the stems to the ground and cover the rows for four or six inches on each side with two or three inches of rough manure. As the spring returns, renew the same process of cultivation to keep down weeds the second year exactly as was done for the first, and so on till the fall of the second year when they may be placed in the forcing house.

To compensate for the loss of a year in time in thus growing asparagus from the seed, such crops as cabbage, lettuce, onions, beets or spinach, all of which will be marketed before the asparagus will have grown enough to interfere with them, can be sown or planted between the rows of asparagus the first year of its growth with but little injury to it; and as the ground for the asparagus has been heavily manured and well prepared, such crops will, in a measure, make up for the year's loss in time.

In some localities, the asparagus beetle has done great injury, causing whole plantations to be plowed under. When the beetle first appears it may be controlled by picking it off and destroying it; but if allowed to become established the task is hopeless. Whenever the eggs appear, cut and burn the plants as long as any traces of the insect are to be seen; this must be done if it destroys every vestige of vegetation. A remedy much in use in some sections is to coop up hens in the vicinity of asparagus beds and let the chicks go out to pick up the larvæ and insects.

A certain remedy against the asparagus beetle, it is claimed, can be made by mixing one pound of Paris green in 100 gallons of water, sprinkling over the plants twice each week on the first appearance of the insect.

PACKING ASPARAGUS

For shipping is best packed in boxes of a depth equal to the length of the bunch or perhaps an inch deeper, because in packing, asparagus is placed on end, and some soft material, as moss, cotton or soft paper should be placed on top, so that should the box be turned upside down, the soft tops will not be injured. The interstices between should also be filled in, so that the whole may be firm enough to not be injured by jarring.

CHAPTER VIII.
EGG-PLANT.

THE egg-plant of our gardens is a native of North Africa. It was first introduced into England in 1596, but for a long time was little known or used, owing much to the climate being unsuited to the perfect development of the fruit. In India and other hot countries it is a favorite article of food, and for many years it has steadily grown in favor in this country. In India it is served up with sugar and wine, and in Italy and France it is used in stews and soups.

* " The possibility of forcing egg-plants successfully was suggested by a crop which was grown under glass in one of the market gardens, near Boston, in the spring of 1891. These plants were not grown with the intention of forcing them ; but as the greenhouse was vacant at the time the main crop of egg-plants was set out of doors, it was filled with plants taken from the same lot as those set in the field. The beds in which they were set were solid, that is, the prepared soil rested on the surface of the ground forming a layer from twelve to fifteen inches in depth. During the preceding year those beds

---
Bul. 96 of C. U.

had served for growing lettuce and they had consequently been well enriched with stable manure, a fertilizer which is especially effective in the production of rapid growth. In July, when the plants grown under glass were compared with those planted in the open ground, an astonishing difference could be observed. Those set in the house were twice as large as the others. The leaves were larger and the stems thicker than those generally found in the gardens of this latitude, and the abundance of healthy foliage was ample proof that the plants were subjected to conditions extremely favorable to their growth. Another interesting point was soon noticed. Although the plants were blooming quite freely, still comparative little fruit had set, and it appeared as if the entire energies of the plant had been directed toward the production of foliage at the expense of the fruit. This condition may be ascribed to two causes:

"Extreme activity of the vegetative functions of plants is often carried on at the expense of fruit production; this fact is commonly illustrated by young fruit trees which blossom several years before they set any fruit. The growth of the egg-plants mentioned above was sufficiently luxuriant to suggest the possibility of its having some effect upon the fruiting powers of the plants. The second and most probable cause of this unsatisfactory fruiting may have been imperfect pollination. Insects and especially bees, were not working so freely in the house as outside, and later experience has shown very clearly that in order to get a satisfactory crop from eggplants grown under glass, thorough pollination must be practiced. The foliage was so dense that the flowers were for the most part hidden. In such a position they were necessarily surrounded by a damp atmosphere, especially when borne upon branches that were near the surface of the soil, and this would still further tend to interfere with the free transfer of pollen by natural agencies. Under such conditions a profitable yield could hardly be expected; yet when carefully observed, the plants proved to be so full of suggestions regarding the proper method of treating them, they should have repaid the time given to their culture by a plentiful harvest of ideas, if not of fruits.

"Acting on the above hints several attempts have been made to grow egg-plants in forcing houses, with the object, however, of fruiting them out of season. The first lot of seed was sown August 30, 1893. It embraced the following varieties: Black Pekin, New York Improved, Early Dwarf Purple, Round Purple and Long White. The seed was sown about three-eights of an inch deep in rich potting soil. The flats or shallow boxes, which contained the seed were placed in a warm house, and the after treatment was very similar to that commonly followed in the growing of tomatoes.

"The seedlings required pricking out about four weeks after the seed was sown. They were set in 2½ inch pots, where they remained until November 14th, when they were shifted into 4 inch pots. On December 17th, or nearly six weeks from the time of seed sowing, the plants had filled these pots with roots, and they were again shifted, but this time into benches. They were set two feet apart each way. The soil was about six inches deep and different in character in each of the two benches used. One bench had been filled with a mixture of equal parts of potting soil and manure from a mushroom bed. This formed a very rich and open soil which appeared to be capable of producing a strong growth. The second bench received a rich, sandy loam, which had previously been composted with about one-fourth its bulk of stable manure. The temperature of the house was that usually maintained in growing plants requiring a considerable amount of heat; during the night the mercury fell to 65° and in the day time it stood at 70°–75°. In bright weather the house was still warmer.

Considerable care was exercised in watering the plants, the soil being kept somewhat dry;

when grown out of doors egg-plants withstand drought so well that such a course seemed advisable when growing them under glass. As the plants increased in size the leaves shaded the soil, and an occasional thorough watering maintained an excellent condition of moisture in the bed filled with the loam. In addition, the soil was stired with a hand weeder when necessary.

For some time, all the varieties seemed to be doing uniformly well, but the plants set in the sandy loam made a stronger growth and appeared to be more vigorous. This was especially noticeable in the Early Dwarf Purple and the New York Improved. The first bloom appeared on the former during the last week in December, and on the 3d of January, 1894. Several plants showed flowers that were well opened. These were hand pollinated and they set fruit freely. On February 15th, some of these fruits were 2½ inches long, the plants still growing well and producing many blossoms. It was at this time that the first flowers of Black Pekin appeared, but New York Improved had not yet produced any, although it was making a strong growth. Round Purple and Long White were making a very slow and weak growth.

On May 29th, the one plant of Early Dwarf Purple had on it 21 fruits of varying sizes, and appeared to be strong enough to mature fruits from beds that were still forming. The larger fruits were four inches in diameter, and nearly six inches long. They were not removed as soon as grown, as should be done in order to get as large a yield as possible, and for this reason the product of the plant is the more remarkable. All the fruits did not attain the size mentioned above for the crop was too heavy for the plant to mature it properly; neither were all the plants of this variety equally prolific, although their yield in many cases closely approched the above. This variety proved to be by far the most promising of those grown for forcing purposes, and it appears to be capable of producing crops which rival those grown out of doors. It is also the earliest variety of those tested, a point which is of the greatest importance. This vegetable is slow in coming into maturity even under the most favorable circumstances.

New York Improved was a very strong grower, and produced large, handsome fruits. Unfortunately, but few could be obtained from a plant, and the total yield was therefore comparatively small, only four or five maturing on the best plants. It is also considerably later than the Early Dwarf Purple.

Black Pekin, on the whole, closely resembled the preceding, especially in the manner of its growth. But it set scarcely any fruit, and that was so late that none were matured before ten months from the time of sowing the seed.

Long White proved to be a weak grower of very slender habit. It is also very late, the fruits being scarcely over two inches in length May 29th. The plants of this variety were slightly checked when young, and this may have been a certain influence in delaying the maturity of the crop, although the effect was probably not very great. One desirable feature of this variety is its smooth foliage which appeared to be unfavorable for the development and presistence of some of the insects that attack greenhouse plants. But the lateness of the variety and the few fruits produced by it will prevent it from being profitably grown under glass.

Round Purple proved to be the most unsatisfactory grower. All the plants showed symptoms of being in unfavorable quarters, and the test with this variety resulted in total failure.

Later attempts to force egg-plants have been made, although no duplicate of the above experiment has been planned. The crops were started later in the season when more heat and sunlight were present. These trials have thrown light upon some of the doubtful points of former experiments, and have shown what is probably the principal cause of the slow maturing of all the varieties tested, and also the very weak growth of some.

One of the results obtained is of especial interest in this connection. Some Early Dwarf Purple plants were started early in August and some of the seedlings were grown in the greenhouses in which different degrees of temperature were maintained. The plants grown in an intermediate or moderately warm house made but little growth, and were soon stunted and worthless. This showed conclusively that egg-plants require a high temperature for their rapid and vigorous growth. Other plants were placed in each of two warm houses, one of which was shaded by means of a thin coat of whitewash upon the glass. The plants in the other house were exposed to direct sunlight and they were also subjected to a bottom heat of scarcely five degrees. Although the air temperature of the two houses was practically identical, the plants receiving the sunlight grew fully twice as fast as the others and had open blossoms before those in the shaded house showed any buds. When some of the latter were removed into the same favored position they very soon showed a benefit from the change. In this way the plants themselves emphasized the necessity of plenty of sunlight for their development in winter quarters;

and a certain amount of bottom heat, from four to six degrees, is also very beneficial, the temperature at the same time being that of a warm house.

Egg-plants designed for forcing should never be stunted. An important aid to prevent this condition is a soil which is open and still rich in available nitrogen. A rich, sandy loam in which all the ingredients are well rotted is preferable to one having the manure in an undecayed condition. The latter is to open, and is more difficult to maintain a proper supply of moisture. The soil should be sufficiently open to afford good drainage, but not so coarse that it dries out too rapidly.

The bench mentioned at the beginning of the article as containing manure from a spent mushroon bed did not prove so satisfactory as the one containing the sandy loam, largely, because it was more difficult to manage.

Another point not to be overlooked in forcing egg-plant is the pollination of the flowers.

Egg-plants are subject to all the greenhouse pests, but if care is exercised from the beginning no serious damage need be feared. Aphis is easily overcome by tobacco smoke (as described elsewhere in this volume), while the mealy bug can be overcome by well directed streams of water. The foliage of egg-plants is not easily injured by such applications of water and the insects may be dislodged with impunity as often as they appear. The worst pests of egg-plant foliage are the red spider and the mite. The latter is especially difficult to treat, as it is not so much affected by moisture as is the red spider, and for this reason can not be so easily overcome. The rough foliage of the egg-plant is especially well adapted to the lodgement of these mites, and when they have once become established their extermination is practically impossible. Too much care, therefore, cannot be taken in watching for the first appearance of these scourges, and in destroying them as soon as discovered. It is well to apply water freely to the foliage, even before the insects appear, for the leaves do not immediately show their presence and such applications will do no harm. The Long White does not suffer from these insects so much as the other varieties, since it has comparatively smooth leaves which do not afford a very secure retreat. Nevertheless it will bear watching as well as the others. The water that is used should be directed mainly toward the under surface of the leaves, as the insects are here found in the greatest abundance, and the parts are also most difficult to reach.

The returns to be derived from egg-plants grown in greenhouses cannot yet be estimated, since to my knowledge no such products have ever been placed upon the market. The first fruits from the south command a good price, but whether the greenhouse article will meet with such favor that it will repay the cost of the long period of growth cannot be told. The experiment from a commercial standpoint is worth trying."

CHAPTER IX.
CELERY, PEAS AND BEANS.
CELERY.

IT has been found that celery cannot be forced as much as other vegetables. It has a tendency to run to seed when grown in hot houses. Celery can, however, be forwarded so as to be ready for market in May and June. At this season of the year there is but a very small amount of celery in market, the stored supply being exhausted and the field product does not mature until some time in July. In order to have celery suitable for market at this season of the year, the seed should be sown early in the winter, or late fall, as it requires a long time for the plants to mature. The plants for two or three months take up but very little room, as the flats can be set in vacant places.

About fifty days after the seed are sown, the plants should be transplanted into other flats, allowing each plant about six square inches. They are left in these flats about thirty days, when they are set in permanent beds that have been occupied by lettuce, radishes or some other winter crop.

The temperature of the house should be kept low, and if the plants can be set in solid beds where there is no bottom heat, so much the better. After the plants have been in their permanent quarters, for about sixty or seventy days, they will be ready to bleach.

This is the most difficult part of the work, as they rot at the least provocation. About the only thing suitable for bleaching is heavy wrapping paper. The stalks are tied together, and a width of paper reaching nearly to the top of the plants, is rolled tightly around them. As the plant grows, another width of paper is rolled about the first, and again reaching nearly to the top of the plant. From thirty to fifty days are required for bleaching.

The Kalamazoo celery is well adapted to house cultivation. The quality of this house-grown product is equal to that grown out of doors, and should be in good demand.

BEANS.

One of the best secondary greenhouse crops is the bean. From forty to sixty days after the seed are sown, the beans are ready for market. The seed should be planted in three-inch pots, two or three beans in each pot, and transplanted in the benches as soon as the roots fill the pots. The bench should contain eight or ten inches of rich, moist soil. The soil should never be allowed to become dry, and especial care must be taken to apply enough water to keep the bottom of the soil moist, and yet not enough to make the surface muddy. With bottom heat the soil is apt to become dry beneath. A house for forcing beans should be light, and the benches should be near the glass. The return heating pipes should be placed under the bench, and the space beneath the bench should be boarded up, so as to confine the heat to the bottom of the bed.

The temperature of a bean house should never fall below 60°. In order to secure a large crop of tender pods, the growth should be rapid from the start. Applications of liquid manure, about once a week, will be very beneficial. Artificial pollination is not necessary, as the bean is "seef-fertile." Any variety that has a compact and rapid growth, and produces long, straight symmetrical pods, is suitable for forcing.

For market the beans are sorted and tied in bunches of fifty pods. These bunches bring varying prices, but from twenty-five to fifty cents may be considered as the average. At these figures, with a good demand, forced beans pay well. The enemies are few—red spider being the worst, and this is kept in check by maintaining a moist atmosphere.

As with all other winter gardening, success depends on having new plants to take the place of the old ones, and thus not loosing any time. It is not profitable to allow the plants to stand after three or four pickings have been made. They should be pulled up, the beds forked over, adding a liberal quantity of strong manure, and new plants immediately set out.

PEAS.

The growing of peas in the greenhouse cannot be advised from a financial standpoint, owing to the small amount produced from a given area.

Peas, when grown under glass, are very sensitive to heat, and the warm, sun-shining days of spring, check their growth to a marked degree. The most healthy and rapid growth is made during the winter months.

For the benefit of those who wish to experiment with peas under glass, we quote the following from bul. 96 of Cornell University: " During the past few years, peas have, at various times, been grown in the forcing houses at Cornell with the intention of determining their value as a commercial crop, and also to study their behavior under glass. The forcing of peas has been carried on in northern Europe for many years, although on a somewhat different plan than that undertaken at this station. Foreign gardeners generally grow the winter crop in frames or hot-beds. In the neighborhood of

Paris such protection is unnecessary, and successive sowings are made in the open air from November to March, one of the most popular varieties for this purpose being St. Catherine. This variety is particularly well adapted to late fall and early winter sowings. In more northern latitudes, either cold frames or hot-beds supply the necessary protection for maturing the crop. Ringleader, Early Dwarf Frame, and Caractacus have been very popular in England. The second named variety is especially adapted for growing in hot-beds. It is exceedingly dwarf, and matures very quickly, so that considerable quantities of peas may be harvested from a small area. Taller varieties are generally bent over to admit of their proper growth.

"Peas thrive in a cool temperature, and the protection afforded by comparatively little glass or wood is sufficient to carry them through moderately cold weather. In the northern states artificial heat must be given if the crop is to be grown during the winter months. As this cannot be done conveniently in frames, larger structures must be employed, and these may be easily supplied with the proper amount of heat for growing this vegetable. A night temperature of 40° to 50°, and a day temperature ten to twenty degrees higher, will be sufficient to cause rapid growth and fairly prolific plants. Peas succeed best, as a rule, if grown in solid beds of rich, sandy soil that is well supplied with water. If peas grown under glass are subjected to the above conditions, their culture presents no serious difficulties, and it will scarcely be necessary to mention details of more than one crop which we have grown. Seeds of two varieties of peas were sown Jan. 6, 1894; they were Extra Early Market and Rural New Yorker. They were planted at the same depth as in outdoor culture, but the seeds were sown more thickly, and the rows were as close to each other as the after culture would allow. Very dwarf varieties, such as Tom Thumb and American Wonder, may be planted in rows three to five inches apart, depending on the richness of the soil, and the general care given the plants. Tall growing varieties, as Champion of England, may be sown in rows running in pairs, the distance between the rows of each pair being from six to ten inches, while the pairs are separated by spaces fifteen to eighteen inches wide. This will allow working room among the plants and still admit of heavy planting.

"One of the essential points in the successful growing of peas, whether in the greenhouse or out of doors, is the use of fresh seed. Garden peas retain their vitality from three to eight years, but the shorter period may be considered as more nearly correct when applied to peas which are to be forced, since the loss of a week or two under glass is expensive, and two sowings cannot be afforded. The seedlings began to appear eight days after seed sowing, and they grew vigorously from the start. February 23d, Rural New Yorker showed first open blossoms, Extra Early Market at the same time having buds that were about to open.

"On the 20th of March, or about seventy-three days from sowing of seed, both varieties had matured sufficient to supply pods that were fit for market, but no picking was made until eleven days later, when the plants yielded pods at the rate of six and one-half quarts for each thirty feet of double row. There was practically no difference between the two varieties as regards to earliness or the amount of yield obtained. Two weeks later a second and last picking was made, the plants yielded only one-half as much as before. This brings the total yield to a little over a peck. This is scarcely a profitable crop, especially since the varieties grown are quite tall and required a trellis.

"Formerly the trellises used consisted of branches forced into the ground so that they would afford support to the vines. But with the crop here considered, a more satisfactory trellis was made by using a wire netting having large meshes. This was fastened between the rows by means of stakes, and then each strip of netting served as a support for a double row. This forms the neatest and most substantial trellis here used for supporting the vines

"The yields from extremely dwarf varieties, such as Tom Thumb, have proved unsatisfactory. The plants require no support, but they yield only one picking and this is so light that their culture under glass cannot in all cases be advised."

CONSTRUCTION

OF

FORCING HOUSES.

SUB-IRRIGATION

AND

THE WATER BENCH.

CHAPTER X.

LOCATION OF THE HOUSE AND CONSTRUCTION OF THE WALLS.

FIRST let us consider the location. This will depend to a great extent on the contour of the land where the house is to be built. In locating the house or houses, means of drainage, especially for the boiler pit, should first be considered. The width and height of the different structures, and the shape of the roofs will have much to do in determining the *exact* location. Where the houses are not connected together in the ridge and furrow fashion, they should be built far enough apart so as to leave a driveway between them. Generally speaking a side hill, sloping to the south is to be preferred, especially for the three-quarter span houses. A level spot is most desired for an even span house. Three-quarter span houses may be built in parallel lines running east and west, the even span houses may run in either direction—east and west or north and south.

Where side ventilation is not desirable, the houses, in my opinion should be built in the ridge and burrow style. This saves lumber, time and expense in building the walls; it also saves land and is more economic in heating and operating the houses.

The potting and working rooms should be located in a position accessible to all of the houses, and the packing room should be arranged so as to facilitate in getting up the orders.

"In locating the various workrooms for a large establishment, it is well to have them in the center, with the houses running from both sides, east and west. A similar arrangement for the heating plant is also desirable: thus, rather than have the boiler room at one end of a long range of houses, the boiler-house could be placed in the center, and houses of half the length arranged on each side and better results obtained."

THE WALLS.

No small amount of time, care and expense should be expended in building greenhouse walls, they are, in most cases, neglected, and the result is that after five or six years they begin to tumble down, often causing considerable loss. The walls may be constructed of wood, brick, stone, grout, or of a combination of material.

WOODEN WALLS.

It is estimated that nine-tenths of the greenhouses at the present time have wooden walls. In their erection, posts of some double material, such as red cedar, locust or cypress, are placed in a straight line four feet apart. The posts should be set three or four feet deep in the ground, and unless the ground is quite firm and solid, a flat stone should be placed under the post, and the hole filled up with dirt and stone, firmly packed. This will hold the post firmly in its place and have a tendency to preserve it. The size of the posts should vary from four by four inches for low walls and narrow houses, to six by six inches for high walls and wide houses. The length will, of course, depend upon the desirable height of the walls. Inch boards, of almost any description, are nailed on the outside of the posts, care being taken to have the boards well matched. In our own houses we have used hemlock exclusively, and it has given perfect satisfaction. On the outside of these boards is tacked some kind of heavy building paper. For the outer covering the patent drop siding will be found preferable to almost any other kind. It is not necessary in vegetable forcing houses to ceil up the posts on the inside; but if this is done the intervening space should not be filled up with sawdust or any other material, as this will absorb moisture and cause a rapid decay of the walls. When the walls are ceiled on the inside they often become an harbor for mice and rats, thus proving to be an injury instead of a benefit.

BRICK WALLS.

Brick walls are not very desirable, as the action of frost and moisture make them comparatively short lived. When brick walls are built, the very hardest brick that can be obtained should be used, as they will not disintegrate or crumble so easily as the softer ones.

A solid brick wall should never be built in a greenhouse as it will radiate the heat very rapidly. There should be at least one air space in it. Two tiers of brick, with one inch of an air space, making a nine inch wall, will answer for a low house. The tiers should be firmly tied together every fourth course vertically, and every three or four bricks along the wall. In the walls of high houses a post should be put in every eight or ten feet, and a third tier of bricks on the inside of the wall, extending one-half or two-thirds the height of the wall, will strengthen it considerable.

MASONRY WALLS.*

The use of stone or grout (cement, sand and cobble stones) for the construction of the foundation of brick walls, is very common, and, as they make a durable wall, would, no doubt, be largely used up to the plates, were it not that they were rapid conductors of heat. In small greenhouses, where the grade can be carried up to the

---

*L. R. Taft's Greenhouse Construction p. 24.

plate, so that none of the wall is exposed to the outside air, they make excellent walls.

The excavation should be to a depth of three feet below the proposed outside grade level, and of a width to admit of a fifteen or eighteen inch footing course. This should occupy the trench up to the level of the interior of the house, at any rate, and even if brick or other material is used for the upper part of the wall, may extend to the level of the ground outside, which is from two to five feet above that of the interior. Stone conducts heat quite rapidly, and for that reason will not be desirable for a wall above ground, unless made very thick. This objection does not hold to the same extent with grout, and where small stones can be readily obtained, it makes a cheap and very durable wall. For a house not over twenty-five feet wide, and when less than five feet in height, a wall of grout twelve inches thick will answer. This should rest on an eighteen inch footing course of the same material. The matérials required are, stones from two to four inches in diameter, gravel and water lime. In making the wall, a box of the desired width is made by driving stakes along the line of the wall on each side, and setting up twelve inch planks for the sides of the box. In this a layer of stones is placed, which should be packed in carefully, and kept, at least, one-half inch from the planks. The cement is then prepared by thoroughly mixing one part with three parts gravel, and then adding enough water to thoroughly moisten it. The best results are obtained, if it is about the same consistency as ordinary lime mortar. The water should not be added until the gravel and cement have been mixed. A layer of cement from two to three inches thick over the stones will be sufficient; this should be well tramped down, filling all of the space between the stones. Another layer of cement and stones can then be added, and the process repeated until the box is filled, requiring about three layers. One wall of the house can be built at a time, although if planks are at hand it will be well to allow one to set while a course is being put in the other. After the grout has been setting for five or six hours, the plank may be raised their own width, and the box will thus be prepared for another course. In this way a wall of any desired height can be built, which will be quite durable and in every way satisfactory.

THE GUTTER AND ROOF.

When the houses are built in the ridge and furrow style, a board, (cypress is generally used) two inches thick and ten or twelve inches wide, is placed on top of the wall to carry off the water.

The top of the wall should be made perfectly smooth, with a slope of about two inches in every one hundred feet. If the gutter will not hold all the water coming from the roof, holes may be made in the bottom and the water carried off by means of tile.

When the houses are not connected together, and on the outside wall of the outer house in the range, a simple plate may be used. In this case the top of the wall is made to have the same angle as the roof.

"In some cases a wooden wall built in exactly the same way as the wall of a dwelling house, is prefered to the 'post and board wall.' For this, a foundation of stone, brick or grout, extending to the outside grade line, is necessary, and an excellent plan is to have two, or even three feet of the wall below this level, with a corresponding excavation for the house, necessitating the erection of a wooden wall of the same height above. In this way the exposed surface is greatly reduced, and a durable and warm wall will be secured. The sill for this wall should be a two by four inch scantling, with studding of the same size, placed two feet apart. The sides and top can be arranged in the same manner as when posts are used. If there is danger of latteral pressure, the sills should be securely anchored to the foundation. This form of wall is especially desirable for narrow houses."

THE ROOF.

The old style of roof was to make a frame of rafters and heavy ridge pole. The glass being placed in ordinary hot-bed sash and the sash placed on the rafters. Every alternate sash being fastened with a hinge and used as a ventilator. The other sash were fastened permanently to the ridge pole and plate or gutter, thus making a tight roof.

The newer and better form of roof is constructed of "permanent sash bars." There is quite a number of patent bars, many of them are made of iron, but the old wooden sash bar is still preferred for commercial houses, while the sash bars in some of the best modern houses are identical with those in use thirty years ago.

It is desirable to have the sash bars made with a gutter on each side so as to catch the condensed moisture, and prevent it from dripping on the plants. During the dull months of mid-winter, the drip falling on a crop of lettuce often causes what is known as lettuce rot. This disease will completely ruin a bed of lettuce in a very short time.

The sash bars should be made of cypress, as it is the strongest and most durable wood that can be had. Ordinary white pine is quite often used, but if it is neglected and not painted once or twice each year it will soon decay.

Cypress is also more stiff and straighter grained, and sash bars can be made smaller, thus letting more light in the house. "While many houses are built without rafters, the sash bars being all of one size, the usual forcing-house construction is to have every fifth sash bar of the nature of a rafter, either two by four inches, or in large houses, two by five inches. The ventilators are then placed in a continuous row on one, or both sides of the ridge, occupying a space of fifteen to thirty inches wide, each sash extending from one rafter to the next. When this method is used, a two by four inch header is mortised into the rafters just under the lower edge of the ventilator, and the sash bars fitted into this, at their upper end, the lower end being nailed to the wall plate."

In my own estimation, and the method that has been followed in building our houses, is to have all of the sash bars to run from the ridge pole to the gutter, or plate, thus letting in more light by dispensing with the heavy rafters. Short headers are placed between the sash bars, instead of the long ones between the rafters. These short headers should be grooved to receive the glass on the lower side. Not many of the general lumber working factories have the necessary machinery for making the deep grooves in the sash bars and crevices in the headers, so it will be necessary to obtain them from some firm dealing in greenhouse material.

I know of no better firm than the Lockland Lumber Co., Lockland, Ohio. We have purchased considerable of greenhouse material from them, and know them to be perfectly honest and reliable. (See their ad. in the back part of this volume.)

IRON HOUSES.

We have not had any experience with "Iron Houses," but we do not think them suitable for vegetable forcing for various reasons. For the benefit of those who desire to build iron houses, we quote the following from L. R. Taft's "Greenhouse Construction." He says:

"For many years houses built entirely of iron and glass, have been used in Europe, and they are now frequently built in this country. In favor of these houses it is claimed that they are almost indestructible, and that, if the iron is galvanized, there will be no necessity for painting the houses. In some cases, zinc or copper is used for the sash bars, and the same claims are made for those houses. For the most part, these claims are true, and although one could afford to pay an increased price for iron houses that would need no outlay for repairs or renewal, provided everything else is desirable. There are several serious objections to iron houses, that have for the most part, restricted their use to large conservatories, and, even there, the combined wood and iron construction is fairly holding its own.

"The objections may be stated as follows:

"1st. As iron is a rapid conductor of heat, the amount thus taken from the house by the iron sash bars will be, perhaps, three to five times as great as would be the case were the wooden sash bars of the same size used, and this requires a noticeable increase in the amount of fuel consumed. Several builders of iron houses, however, have so reduced the amount of iron exposed to the outer air, that, so far as radiation is concerned, there is, perhaps, no great difference.

"2d. With several of the methods of glazing, the packing used, although tight at first, soon becomes loose and allows the heated air to pass through the cracks.

"3d. Even if the roof is water tight, there will be a large amount of water congealed on the under side of the sash bars at night, which, melting as the heat rises in the morning, causes quite a shower. (This would be very detrimental to vegetable forcing.) Frequently, in systems where large glass is used, a metallic strip is placed between the panes to act as a gutter to catch the moisture condensed on the glass. If it works all right there should be no drip from the glass, but they finally become clogged.

"4th. Even if such is not the case in England, it is found, in our extremes of temperature, that unequal expansion and contraction sometimes crack the large panes, unless everything is very carefully adjusted, so that there is more or less broken glass.

"These objections have more force with the sash bars used for skylight glass, in conservatories, and do not hold true to the same extent when used for smaller panes in forcing houses. In conservatories, however, although the drip is not desirable, it does far less injury than in houses used for forcing and growing plants, and one will need to place the greater durability and cheapness of maintenance of the metal roofs against the acknowledged increase of fuel required to heat the houses. The use of iron sash bars with metallic glazing, for commercial forcing houses, has not become general, as the matter of drip and of fuel, to say nothing in the increased first cost of the houses, are questions of considerable moment."

The use of iron posts and rafters has been for some time, and their use is becoming more and more into general practice. The question of durability should receive more attention than it has in the past. There can be no question but that, in the construction of greenhouses, in the future iron will be quite largely used.

"Various methods of construction are now in use, one of the best combining a framework of iron with wooden sash bars. For forcing houses, the rafters are about three by one-half inch, and are surmounted by a wooden rafter cap. The rafters are fastened to each other and to the ridge, by iron knees or brackets. The purlines are of one and one-half inch to two inch angle iron, and are fastened to the rafters by means of iron lugs. If desired, gas pipe purlines can be used. With large glass, and small sash bars, the purlines should be quite close together, but as the size of the glass decreases, they may be further apart. While four feet will not be none too little in one case, they may be as much as eight feet in the other. When the ventilators are in long rows, on either side of the ridge, the upper line of purlines should be under the lower edge of the sash, and should carry a wooden header, into which the upper ends of the sash bars are mortised. To the other purlines the sash bars are fastened by means of wood screws."

"When the distance between the rafters or other supports is not over six or seven feet, one-inch gas pipes will make quite a stiff roof. They can be inserted in holes in wooden rafters when these are used, or can be held up by means of small castings attached to iron rafters. When the roof is constructed of sash bars, without the use of rafters, a continuous line of pipe supported by posts, at intervals of six feet, will form a good purline. The pipe may be cut in lengths of six feet, and screwed into the tees to which the posts are attached, or, what is perhaps easier to put up, the tees are reamed out, so as to allow the pipe to slip through them. The lengths are screwed together, and, if desired, can be used as water pipes. If the purline is connected by screw-joints with one or more of the posts on each side, a hose can be attached, and, although the effect will not be lasting, the water in the pipes will have the chill taken off. When a pipe purline is used, with supports more than eight feet apart, it does not give good satisfaction, as it is more or less liable to sag. In order to hold the sash bars firmly down on the purlines, iron clips can be used, which should be screwed to at least every other sash bar."

In houses less than fifteen feet wide, with a walk in the center, no center posts need be used, if the wall posts are set firm, especially if a truss bracket is used in the angle of the roof, there will be no danger of its sagging. As the width of the house increases more support is necessary. In modern houses that are over fifteen feet wide, the ridge should be supported by means of a row of one inch or one and one-fourth inch gas pipe. These posts should be placed every ten or twelve feet. If the rafters are more than nine feet long, they should be supported in the center by another row of posts.

In wide houses a purline should be placed every six feet, and every purline should be supported by a row of posts.

When it is desirable to have the center bed elevated, when possible, the purline posts should be placed so as to serve for legs to support it. This can be done by cutting the posts, at the proper height, and inserting tees into which the cross supporters of the bed are screwed. The top end of the posts are screwed into tees in the purline, and the lower ends should be placed on a solid, durable foundation that will hold them securely in their places.

CHAPTER XIII.
GLASS AND GLAZING.

THE glass most commonly used at present, (1896) is known as "A" quality and either "single" or "double" strength. This quality of glass, it is true, is considerable more expensive than the "B," "C" or "D" quality. But it is less likely to burn the plants, and as it will stand a much harder blow, the breakage from hail storms and by accident will be much less, so that it will be cheaper in the end.

In buying glass it should be carefully noted that every box bears the brand of the quality that you contracted for. Choose the boxes that are the least bruised and scuffed, as this indicates that they have been handled with care, and the glass is less liable to be broken than that contained in the. badly damaged boxes. Glass that is of even thickness, flat and free from imperfections that will cause sun-burns, should be used. The imperfections in the glass are caused from air bubbles, unmelted specks, or various impurities. As the substances of which glass is composed are fused together, the impurities settle to the bottom, leaving the glass at the top perfectly clear and transparent. From this the "A" quality is taken, "B" comes from a layer just beneath, and so on down the scale until "D" and "E" are reached, which should never be used on a greenhouse roof. The lower grades are made by poor workmen, and not only are they likely to contain imperfections, but are less even in thickness.

SIZE OF GLASS.

The size of glass used for greenhouse purposes, has been greatly increased within the last few years. A comparatively short time ago, glass as small as five by seven inches was used almost exclusively. But in many houses of to-day we find panes that are twenty-four inches wide. The extremely large glass makes a very light house, well suited to forcing vegetables, but it is generally thought advisable to use a smaller size. The cost of glass, after the size passes eighteen inches in width, increases very rapidly. This not only makes the first cost more, but it also increases the cost of repairs.

I think the best size, for the common forcing-houses, is from twelve to sixteen inches wide, *i. e.*, for the northern states, where there is a heavy snow fall. The weight of the snow is likely to break the wide glass.

GLAZING.

This sould be done with great care, the great desiderata being to make a roof as near air and water proof as possible, and to have the glass fastened securely, so that the wind will not have a tendency to loosen it. I have seen houses, that after a wind storm, nearly one-third of the glass would be blown off and broken.

Nearly all glass is more or less curved, and if two panes in which the curves are not equal are placed together, there is likely to be a crack somewhere, either at the corners or in the center. Therefore, the glass should be sorted, and if the curves are of different angles, those of one angle should be put in one row, and those of another angle put in another row. Until quite recently, the method of glazing, almost universally adopted, was to lap the glass from one-eighth to one-fourth of an inch, the upper pane extending down on the edge of the pane below. The glass was imbedded in putty, and fastened to the sash bar by means of large glazing points, using no putty on top. The glazing points used were triangular, the corner of which was bent down, so that when it was driven in, it would fit against the lower edge of each pane and prevent it from slipping down. It was found that when the glass laid on the sash bars, thus imbedded, the putty soon rots or wears out, and water gets in, and not only loosens the glass, but rots the bar as well. This was obviated by pouring along the junction of the bar with the glass a thin line of white lead in oil, over which is shaken dry white sand. These old methods are rapidly giving way to the newer and more practicable system of

"BUTTED GLASS."

This method of glazing is fast coming into general use. Some of its advantages are as follows:

1st. A tighter roof can be made, thus saving considerable fuel, and lessening the amount of drip.

2d. There is less danger from broken glass, either from ice forming between the panes when lapped, or from accidents, as, when a lapped pane is broken it frequently cracks the one beneath.

3rd. More benefit can be derived from the sun, for when the glass is lapped, soot and dust soon collect between the laps, making an opaque streak, and even when this is not so, the double glass at the lap obstructs more light than the single glass.

4th. When the clipper sash bar is used, butted glass can be put on a roof four or five times as fast as where the old style bar is used, as it does not require any putty or white lead, except between the panes, and many do not even do this. The glass is simply placed on the sash bars, (care being taken not to leave any crack between the panes) and the clipper, or cap is screwed down, thus making the panes perfectly tight, and nothing can loosen them, unless they are broken.

When it is desirable to put putty between the joints, a mixture of equal parts of white lead and putty is spread out in a thin layer on a smooth board. The ends of the glass are then dipped into the mixture and placed on the bar. Each pane should be tried to see if it will fit up close, before it is dipped. There is a patented

GLAZING STRIP,

But it has not, as yet, come into general use. "It consists of a narrow strip of zinc bent into the shape of the letter Z, which is placed between the panes so that one leg of the Z is under the upper panes, and the other leg over the under ones."

The chief objection to these strips, is, that it is necessary to fill the crack between the strip and glass to make a tight joint, thus requiring extra time and labor. But when once properly put together, will make the roof water-tight much longer than when the lead alone is used.

When the strips are not properly laid, and the filling of the cracks is neglected, there will be much more drip than when the strips are not used.

These strips also shut out a small portion of light, but this does not amount to a great deal when the large panes are used.

CHAPTER XIV.
VENTILATORS.

PLANTS, as well as animals, *must* have fresh air. In vegetable forcing it is necessary to have the houses well ventilated, if they are not, success will be impossible.

The air in forcing houses is always, or nearly always, warmer than that on the outside, it naturally ascends, hence ventilators are more effective when placed at the highest part in the building. If an opening is made for the escape of warm air, fresh air will immediately take its place.

Direct drafts of cold air on the plants should be prevented, this can be done by the proper arrangement of the ventilators and heating pipes.

When the ventilators are hinged to the ridge pole, they should be on the opposite side from which the prevailing winds blow. When they are hinged to the headers, they should be on the side against which the prevailing wind blows. Some writers advocate that a row of ventilators be placed on each side of the ridge, those on one side being hinged to the ridge, and those on the other being hinged to the headers, thus if the wind blows in on one side, the ventilation may be given from the other side.

In some houses large ventilators have been placed at intervals along the roof; but much better results are obtained when only one sash bar is left between the ventilators, thus making almost a continuous ventilator. Ventilators thus arranged will give more ventilation than where there is a continuous row.

THE SASH.

The sash are made similar to hot bed sash, the bars running crosswise instead of lengthwise. The glass used for the sash should be of the same width as that used for the rest of the house, so that the bars in the sash will lay directly over the sash bars.

SASH LIFTERS.

Various styles of machines are used for this purpose. In the majority of them, the power is conveyed by a gas pipe shaft, running lengthwise of the house near the ventilators. The shaft is factened either to the ridge posts, rafters or sash bars, by means of small hangers. The power is applied to the sash by means of elbows, one end of which is fastened to the shaft and the other end to the sash.

"Of the machines used to work the shafting, with its elbow fixtures, the simplest is the kind generally used by greenhouse builders. It con-

VENTILATORS.

sists of a large wheel upon the shaft, worked by a worm upon the upper end of a rod, to which the power is applied by means of a crank, or hand wheel."

The "Standard," manufactued by E. Hippard, Youngstown, Ohio, is a very easy machine to operate, and has given us good satisfaction. We have used no other in our houses at Hanging Rock, Ohio. It is stated that, in the old machines, the large wheel on the shaft sometimes slipped, or was pushed away from the pinion, but with the new double header this is impossible. The power is applied, by means of a hand wheel or worm to the vertical shaft which works inside the post. At the upper end of the shaft is a pinion, by which the power is conveyed to the shaft.

CHAPTER XV.
BENCHES AND BEDS.
BENCHES.

THE best greenhouse benches are made of iron and tile, or slate, but the average Vegetable Forcer thinks that he cannot afford to go to this expense, he therefore puts up wooden structures, which are a constant source of trouble and expense. Built as they usually are, of cheap or waste lumber, they will not last to exceed four years. It often happens that considerable loss is occasioned by trying to run the benches for a year longer than they will stand. Not only are plants lost, that were on the bench when it succumbed to their weight, but time, labor and money must be expended in the construction of a new bench. With a little attention in constructing and caring for

WOODEN BENCHES,

their durability can be greatly increased.

When wooden legs are used they should be lifted above the soil and walk, upon a brick or stone pile. This will keep the lower end dry, and prevent decay to some extent. Red cedar, locust, cypress, or white pine are suitable for posts, cypress being preferred.

In case the walls of the house are made of wood, one end of the timbers supporting the bench, can be nailed to the posts in the wall. "When the wall cannot be used to support the backs of the side benches, wooden legs can be used the same as for the fronts." These should be about two by four inches square and from two to five and a half feet high, according to circumstances.

Two by four inch scantling is large enough for the cross bearers under narrow benches, that is, when they are not over three feet in width.

For wider benches, the size of the scantling should increase with the width of the bench, side benches, however, should not be over three, or three and one-half feet in width, as they will be inconvenient in setting out the plants. These cross bearers should not be over four feet apart, if the bottom of the bench is to be made of boards. Common six by one inch fencing plank make a very good bottom, placing them close together and by pouring a thin coat of cement over them, the bed will be absolutely water tight, and give good service for quite a number of years. (For further particulars about water-tight benches see chapter on Sub-irrigation.)

When it is possible, we would advise the use of gas pipe for the legs and cross bearers, as they are easily put up, and will last a lifetime. The lower end of the front row of legs are set on locust, or cedar posts. On the upper end of each leg is screwed a tee, into the latteral hole of this tee, one end of the cross bearer is inserted, the other end being fastened to the wall of the house. To support the plank forming the side of the bench, a piece of pipe about six or seven inches long is screwed into the end of the tee. This holds the side board in its place, and prevents it from "warping over." The front boards can, if desired, be placed outside the pipe, and be held in place by iron clips. For the front and back of the benches six inch boards are used.

Greenhouse benches vary in width, to a large degree, with the width of the house. The side benches are sometimes as narrow as two feet, and seldom are wider than three and one-half feet, four feet being the maximum. The center benches range from seven to twelve feet, when they are built up solid from the floor of the house, and are over eight feet wide, a narrow path is made through the center.

SOLID BEDS.

For growing many vegetable crops the solid beds are very desirable, as they hold moisture exceedingly well. They are also very inexpensive. If the underlying soil is loose and sandy, a layer of clay is placed over it and packed down to make it as near water tight as possible.

On top of this is placed six or seven inches of prepared compost. The walls, to keep the soil in place, are made of plank, or brick, one inch boards are preferred, as the brick take up too much space.

CHAPTER XVI.

METHODS OF HEATING.

HAVING completed the "shell" of our house, let us now consider some of the methods of heating. Throughout the northern states, most of the plants grown in the vegetable forcing-house require artificial heat during six or eight months of the year. Some crops thrive best at a temperature of 40° to 50° and will not be injured if exposed to one or two degrees of frost, while others require a temperature of 70° or more. In order to maintain the proper temperature, various methods have been in practice.

The simplest way of producing heat for plant growth, is by slowly decomposing vegetable matter. This, however, is only used in hot beds, and could not be used to heat a greenhouse of any considerable size.

The old smoke flue has answered a good purpose in its day, but "the old must give place for the new." It cost little for construction, but requires considerable of expense to run it, especially in the items of fuel and attendance. In some sections of the country the flue is still made use of in heating small greenhouses, but all the larger commercial houses are heated by steam or hot water.

The hot water system, "was one of the first to be used for the heating of greenhouses in modern times, it is claimed that the circulation of hot water, as a means of conveying heat, was used by the old Romans in heating their dwellings. It went out of use, however, until 1777, when a Frenchman, Bonnemain, re-introduced it. Ancient as the method is, the hot water systems of to-day are comparatively modern inventions, and bear little resemblance to those used even fifty years ago; in fact, the change has been so recent that many of the systems in use to-day are built on quite different principles from those constructed according to the latest ideas."

It is stated that the Romans used circulating pipes made of bronze, and the first pipes used for greenhouse heating were five inches in diameter, these, however, were made of copper. The heaters, or in reality, large open kettles, were also made of copper. These kettles were placed over furnaces, and from them the pipes run to the other end of the house, where they entered a copper reservoir. The pipes forming the flow, left the kettle at the top and the return pipes entered at the bottom.

"The use of steam in closed circuits was invented by Mr. Hague, in England, about 1820, although certain methods in which the steam passed off at the further end of the house, had been previously in use. At this time the construction of apparatus was such as to require almost constant attention to fires in order to maintain the temperature. Frequent repairs were needed and explosions were common."

"The use of steam for heating purposes began to receive marked attention some fifteen years ago. In the discussions of the Society of American Florists, in 1885, the average from estimates in answer to circulars by nearly fifty florists showed that one ton of coal with hot water heated 108 square feet of glass to a temperature of $53\frac{1}{3}$ degrees, while with steam the same amount heated 149 square feet to a temperature of $60\frac{3}{4}$ degrees."

Peter Henderson, in 1885 and 1886, made the first really comparative test of steam and hot water heating. The trial was made with two houses of the same size and construction, one being fitted with a steam boiler and pipes, the other with a hot water outfit. By weight of the coal, it was found that the house heated with steam used twenty-five percent less fuel than the house heat with hot water.

In a pamphlet on greenhouse heating, by A. B. Fowler, steam is considered preferable.

"In 1888 two houses were constructed at the Massachusetts Experiment Station as nearly alike as possible, with boilers of the same make and pattern, one fitted for steam, the other for hot water. The following winter careful observations were made of temperatures and the amount of fuel consumed. The results showed a saving of nearly twenty per cent. of coal in favor of hot water heating, while the average temperature of the house was slightly higher. The temperature was also more uniform in the house heated by hot water. The test was repeated in the following winter and showed a still greater advantage in favor of hot water, there being a saving of over thirty per cent. in the fuel consumed."

CHAPTER XVII.

HEATING BY HOT WATER.

THE BOILER.

HUNDREDS of designs of hot water heaters have been put on the market, and there are several that it is hard to decide which is really superior.

The wrought iron heater is more likely to rust, and is also injured more than cast iron by the sulphurous and other gas that comes from combustion. For these reasons it is claimed by some that cast iron boilers will last much longer than those made of wrought iron. With some boilers this has really been the case, but they were not made of the double strength pipe, of which they should have been. When none of the pipes used are less than one and one-fourth inch, and these made of double strength iron, the durability will be greatly increased.

The boiler should be simple, durable and compact. The direct fire heating surface should be properly arranged and adjusted to the grate area. The water sections and tubes should also have the proper arrangement, so as to facilitate the circulation in the boiler. The boiler should be so constructed that every part can be cleaned without causing extra work in tearing down and putting up the different parts. It should have as near a perfect draft adjustment as possible and the grate should be so arranged as to remove the ashes and clinkers with ease and rapidity. *Every* part of the boiler should be interchangeable or easily repaired.

"The circulation in the heater should be as short as possible, and it is better to have the water spread out in thin sheets, and with the arrangement such that the water is divided into a number of portions, each of which makes a single short circulation, than it is to have the entire mass of water that flows through the heater warmed by convection, or compelled to pass in a zigzag course through a number of different tubes and sections."

So far as circulation is concerned, vertical tubes are preferred to those that are horizontal, as the friction is lessened. But the friction in a horizontal pipe is so small that it is more than counterbalanced by the increasing efficiency of the horizontal fire surface. Boilers that have drop tubes over the fire box, are advantageous for both, vertical circulation and horizontal fire surface. The only objection to this kind of tubes is that the water cannot be drawn from them.

DISTRIBUTING PIPES.

Until quite recently the pipes used to carry the hot water through the house, were made of cast iron, being four inches in diameter and fastened together by means of large shoulders and packed joints, they were very heavy and clumsy to handle. But in the improved hot water system of to-day, the largest pipe used in the coils are not over two inches in diameter, while one and one-fourth and one and one-half inch pipe are used for the short courses.

In the new system the lengths of pipe are about three times as long and can be screwed together, instead of packing every joint. The four inch pipe contains four times as much water as the two inch pipe, yet they only have twice the radiating surface. On account of the large pipe being so heavy it is necessary to place it low down under the benches, just a trifle above the top of the heater, while the small pipe can be carried to the highest part of the house if desired, and thus a far more rapid circulation is maintained.

Advocates for the large pipe, claim that it is safer to use, as it will hold the heat for a longer time, if the fire should be allowed to go out. This is undoubtedly true, but with a well arranged system an even temperature can be maintained with small pipes for ten to twelve hours, on mild winter nights.

NUMBER AND POSITION OF PIPES.

For most commercial establishments it is preferred to have a combination of over-head and under-bench piping; the main or flow pipe being placed over-head near the ridge and under the ventilators; the return pipes being placed under the side benches. By placing one or more of the flows under the ventilators, they warm the cold air to a considerable extent, as it passes over them, thus protecting the plants from cold drafts, when ventilation is given.

If it be desired to use the under-bench system, it will require to heat a house one hundred and fifty feet long and twenty feet wide, having one center and two side benches, a three inch flow and four one and one-half inch returns under each side bench. In a combination of over-head and under-bench piping, about the same amount of pipe is required as for each of the other two methods.

Generally speaking, the rules for the arrangements of pipes can be used in all kinds of houses, modified, of course, to suit the various conditions.

Every flow and return pipe should have a valve, so as to shut a portion of the heat off, on warm days.

THE EXPANSION TANK.

This is a reservoir into which the surplus water runs as it is heated and expands. It should be raised as high as possible, and connected with the mains, by a pipe, in size proportional to the extent of the system. The tank may be made of galvanized iron, without a cover, with the expansion pipe connected at the bottom, and an overflow attached near the top, or a close tank may be used. A regular riveted boiler may be used for this, with the same connections, and also a water gauge and safety valve.

When the closed tank is used it need not be elevated so high, as must the open tank in order to produce the desired pressure.

"The closed tank has the same effect as does the elevated one, and merely raises the point to which the water can be heated without forming steam. One advantage of this is that, when water is carried at 220°, much less heating pipe is required than when it is only 160°, but a serious objection to this is that it now has one of the faults of steam, as, at this temperature, more heat will be carried up the chimney with the products of combustion, than when the water is 180°. It is an excellent plan to have the house supplied with sufficient radiating surface to maintain the required temperature in the average winter weather with an open tank, but to have the system provided with a safety valve, which could be thrown on when it became necessary, in order to keep up the temperature when the thermometer goes down below zero."

CHAPTER XVIII.

HEATING WITH STEAM.

THE advocates for steam heating claim that the first cost of construction is forty per cent less than in the hot water system, this has reference, however, to the old style in which the four inch pipes were used. In systems where the small pipes and closed tank are employed, the cost is not any more, but there is a loss in fuel as it is necessary to maintain a higher pressure.

The steam system should not be used in small establishments where a fireman is not employed both night and day; for if the water in the boiler be allowed to fall below 212°, steam will go down and the pipes immediately cool off, often causing great loss.

PIPING FOR STEAM.

This does not vary to any considerable extent from the small pipe hot water arrangement. As before stated, almost all vegetables thrive best in houses heated by a combination of overhead and under-bench piping. The flow as well as the returns should not have any slight depressions or elevations, but the slope should be uniform

HEATING WITH STEAM.

throughout. All the pipes should slope toward the boiler, in order to return the condensed steam. The returns should be connected to one large pipe which enters the boiler at the bottom. Each strand of return pipe should contain a shut-off valve and an air cock.

AMOUNT OF PIPE.*

The amount of pipe both for mains and coils will be much less than when hot water is used. For the main it can be reckoned that a 1½ inch pipe will supply 200 sq. ft. of radiation. 2 inch pipe will supply 400 sq. ft. of radiation. 2½ inch pipe will supply 800 sq. ft. of radiation. 3 inch pipe will supply 1600 sq. ft. of radiation. 4 inch pipe will supply 3200 sq. ft. of radiation. The surface of the steam pipes is from thirty to forty per cent warmer than that of hot water pipes, and a corresponding decrease of the necessary radiating surface can be made.

For low pressure steam, in addition to the mains, a house will require for each one thousand square feet of glass, to warm it to 45° to 50°, 140 square feet or 300 linear feet 1¼ inch pipe; 50° to 60°, 175 square feet or 400 linear feet 1¼ inch pipe; 60° to 70°, 225 square feet or 500 linear feet 1¼ inch pipe.

With high pressure, a considerable reduction can be made from the above.

---
* Greenhouse Construction by Taft.

In figuring the capacity of a boiler, about fifteen feet of heating (fire) surface should be reckoned as one horse power, and in estimating the radiation it will supply, from fifty to ninety square feet of radiation per horse power, according to the pressure, may be relied upon with a good boiler. If we consider that for a temperature of fifty degrees, which may be taken as about the average, one square foot of radiating surface will take care of six square feet of glass, one horse power will be sufficient for 300 to 540 square feet of glass. As in the case with hot water heaters, a large steam boiler will handle more glass to a square foot of glass than a small one.

The size of grate for a given glass area will also depend upon the draft of the chimney, the skill of the fireman, and the method of stoking used. With a poor draft a much smaller amount of coal can be burned, per square foot of grate, than when the draft is strong, and a grate considerably larger than in the latter case will be required; the same is true of a dirty fire as compared with a clean one. For establishments with less than 10,000 to 12,000 square feet of glass, a night fireman can hardly be afforded, and a large grate should be used upon which a slow fire can be burned that will last from six to ten hours. For this purpose the grate should have an area of from fifteen to eighteen or even twenty feet, according to climate and other modifying conditions. On the other hand, when a strong draft can be secured, and in large establishments, where a night fireman is employed, one square foot of grate will readily handle one thousand square feet of glass. In other words, a steam boiler with twelve square feet of grate can be made to heat with economy 12,000 square feet of glass under favorable conditions, eight square feet of grate will heat a house containing the same amount of glass to fifty degrees.

CHAPTER XIX.

SUB-IRRIGATION.

WITHIN the last few years the watering of greenhouses has been greatly faciliated by means of sub-irrigation. The idea was originated by Mr. W. S. Turner, ex-assistant Horticulturist at the Ohio Experiment Station. His experiments were followed by Mr. Rane of the West Virginia Station.

In order to sub-irrigate the bed should be made solid and water tight, or as nearly so as possible. This can be done by using tongue and ground plank for the bottom of the bed. After the plank has been made secure, they should receive a thick coat of white lead, being thoroughly rubbed into the cracks. Common inch boards may be used by covering them with a thin coat of cement, this makes a very durable bed, and is entirely water tight. When the beds are built up from the ground they can be made water-tight by filling in the bottom with five or six inches of stiff clay, it being thoroughly packed down either by tramping with the feet or pounding with some heavy article. Strings of two inch tile are used to distribute the water through the bed. One end of the last tile in each row is placed on the board forming the end of the bed so as to leave an opening in which to pour the water. The rows of tile should be about two feet apart. When the beds are very wide, the water may be distributed much more evenly, if the tile are run crosswise in the bed, thus making the runs of water short. When the tile is run lengthwise, it requires particular leveling and adjusting of bench and tile line, so that the water will neither rush too freely at first, nor be carried too fast to the further end. One and one-fourth inch gas pipe may be used in place of the tile. Small holes are drilled in the pipe four or five inches apart, alternately on opposite sides. The further end is partially closed by a wooden plug with a small hole through it, on the other end is placed an elbow and funnel to receive the water, or it may be connected directly to the water supply. In this case, when the bed needs water, all that is necessary is to open the valve until the bed is sufficiently wet, which is not any considerable length of time. This is a great saving of labor and expensive. In amateur houses, where the watering is done overhead by the ordinary garden sprinkler, it is a very tedious task. In sub-irrigation we simply pour the water into the funnel, or turn the valve, and the work is not only done, but is done well.

By this method of application we can use any kind of liquid fertilizers we wish, which can not satisfactorily de done by the old over-head method. Where surface irrigation is followed, the beds are never thoroughly wet. Two or three bucket fulls of water sprinkled on in the usual manner, will make quite a large bed appear soaked, while, in fact, the water has not reached beyond an inch in depth, leaving the lower portions without any moisture whatever. This causes the dirt in the bottom of the bed to become so dry and hard that it is impossible for the roots of the plant to penetrate it. Even if they could penetrate it they would not receive any food from soil in this condition, for "all plant food *must* be in a liquid form before it can be assimilated by the plant." On a bed, where one bucket full of water applied to the surface, would render it apparently quite wet, you can turn in five or six bucket fulls through under-ground pipes, without bringing moisture enough for a respectable show to the surface.

Almost every one without exception, would apply a greater quantity of water by sub-irrigation than by the old method of surface watering. This abundant supply of water is what causes the great increase in the growth of certain greenhouse crops observed as the result of sub-irrigation. It is surprising what large quantities of water lettuce will take and delight in. Amateurs never give it enough to promote the most rapid growth possible. With the new arrangement this is different. The application does not quickly show on the surface, and consequently it is naturally more abundant than under the old method. The roots of the plants are kept well supplied with moisture all the time and the growth, therefore, is rapid and healthy.

The effect of sub-irrigation upon the growth of lettuce and radishes is very remarkable, some claim an increase of 50 per cent. On tomatoes the effect is not so marked, although there is quite a noticeable increase in the growth and productiveness. The effect on cucumbers is decidedly beneficial. Sub-irrigated radishes come to a marketable size earlier and are larger than those grown by ordinary method. The difference in earliness is more marked than the total increase in weight. Nearly all of the radishes grown on a sub-irrigated bed, are sold before any of those grown on surface watered beds are ready to pull. The less time required for a crop to mature, the more crops can be taken from the same space during a certain length of time.

Summing up, we have the following in favor of sub-irrigation :—

* 1st. It is the most complete and satisfactory method of watering.

2nd. The surface soil never becomes hardened.

3rd. Beds never dry out or bake on the bottom.

* Market Garden.

4th. The appearance of the bed is not deceiving as is sometimes the case in surface watered beds.

5th. Plants grow more evenly than under the old method.

6th. Fungus diseases are checked, or are entirely prevented.

7th. A great saving of time.

8th. A great saving of labor.

9th. The soil can be worked at all times, and thus kept in better condition.

10th. Less water is required.

11th. The beds require watering once a week, while surface irrigation generally needs it daily.

12th. The yearly expense to keep in repair is very small.

13th. The pipe or tile serves both to water the beds and to retain the excessive moisture.

14th. The openings beneath the soil allow free access of the air; hence the soil never becomes sour or stagnant.

15th. Parsley was ready for market when it was only one-third grown on the surface watered beds.

16th. There was a marked gain in the productiveness of tomatoes.

17th. Long-rooted radishes proved superior.

18th. Lettuce is from 30 to 50 per cent better.

19th Lettuce rot is prevented to a great extent.

20th. Spinach matures earlier.

21st. Cucumbers show a marked increase.

CHAPTER XX.
THE WATER BENCH.

IN my estimation, no greenhouse, especially a vegetable house, is complete unless it has a good water bench.

All growers of plants from seed (that is small seed), know the inconvenience of watering newly sown seed, the greatest care being necessary to avoid washing the cover from the seed and leaving them exposed. It also requires no small amount of skill to water small seedling plants without injury, as it is almost impossible to keep from knocking them over, especially if the watering is done with a hose attached to a hydrant or force pump, or if the ordinary garden sprinkler is used.

It is very undesirable to have the seed "washed out" as it retards germination, in fact, a large amount of seed will not germinate at all unless they are covered. The covering holds moisture and a seed cannot sprout without moisture. This trouble has been overcome by the introduction of The Water Bench, which is simply a water-tight bench, and is constructed on the same plan as benches used for sub-irrigation. Generally speaking, it is just a continuation of a sub-irregated bed, partitioned off by a water-tight partition to keep the soil and water separated. The sides should not be over three or four inches high, this makes it more convenient for handling the flats. It is not necessary to devote any more space to the water bench than is required for seed recently sown, and young plants in flats, nor is it needful to have the bench located in the best part of the house. The water bench may be placed under a bed of growing plants, this does very well for seed flats, but plants will not live very long in the dark. The best is to construct a water bench in a part of the house that is to be devoted to young plants, and immediately under the first bench put in another of the same dimensions.

The second, or lower bench, is to be used for germinating seeds, and little or no light is required. A space of about twelve or fifteen inches should be left between the benches, so as to give plenty of room to pass the flats in and out easily.

When it is necessary to water the flats containing newly sown seed, or young plants just transplanted, or plants too small to be pricked off, they are transfered to the water bench, which should have about three inches of water in it, and allowed to remain until they are thoroughly soaked, but not long enough for the soil to become mortar-like or pasty.

The flats in which seeds are sown may be kept in the lower bench until the seed germinates and the young plants appear, but should not be kept in the dark after this for any length of time, as loss would surely be the result. In the upper water bench plants may be kept as long as desired, and watered as often as need be. But by moving the flats from the bench as soon as they are thorougly wet, a smaller water bench can be used.

This method of watering young plants and seed flats is very satisfactory as it saves labor and prevents injury. Not only can the soil be thoroughly and evenly watered is this manner, but there is no danger of washing out the seed, nor knocking over young plants. This method is especially applicable to small and delicate seeds.

The water bench may also be used for watering cabbage plants, strawberry plants, tomato plants, etc., for outdoor purposes. Even if there is a large number to be watered it can be done about as cheap, if not cheaper, than by the old method, and most undoubtedly is more thorough. In the summer time it is quite difficult to germinate seeds successfully where surface watering is practiced, but by this plan success is certain.

PART III.

HOT BEDS
AND
COLD FRAMES.

CHAPTER XXI.
HOT BEDS.

HOT beds, although I do not consider them near so economical or convenient in the long run as forcing-houses, play an important part with the amateur, who, as a general rule, is not over-supplied with money. Therefore, as the first cost of construction is so much less than that for forcing houses, they are his only or chief resort. Not only is the material used in their construction inexpensive, but they are so simple in structure, that it is not necessary to employ a carpenter, and pay him three or four dollars per day, to build them. Any man with ordinary intelligence is carpenter enough to put them together.

LOCATION.

The selection of the site for the hot-beds is of no small importance. They should be built in as warm a place as can be found, that is within convenient distance from the dwelling, or greenhouses if there be any. A south or southeasternly slope, is desirable, especially if there is a natural protection from the northwest winds. If there is no natural protection, it will be necessary to build a tight board fence, not less than six feet high, on the north and west sides of the beds. But if it so happens, that there is a close, tall hedge, or buildings of any description, that stand in such a position as to be used for protection, so much the better.

Another thing to be considered, is the character of the soil on which the beds are to be built. If it is not loose and dry, *i. e.*, having a natural drainage, artificial means should be resorted to.

USES OF HOT-BEDS.

The chief purpose for which hot-beds are constructed, is the production of plants for early spring planting, when a supply has not been wintered over in the cold frames. Hot-beds are, also, used for various other purposes, of which the forcing of lettuce is the most important. During the spring months this crop is generally scarce, and good prices are commended. Very often the first crop of hot-bed lettuce brings about three dollars per sash.

The first crop is planted in the bed, fifty plants under each sash, about the first week in January. This crop will mature the first week in March, when another crop can be planted; the second crop will not be so profitable as the first, however, as the crop from cold frames will be in market by the time it has come to marketable size.

Radishes, cucumbers and beets can also be profitably grown in hot-beds.

CONSTRUCTION.

The ordinary method is to dig a trench two and one-half feet deep, seven feet wide, and as long as it is desired to have the bed. The beds should all have the same dimensions, so that the sash from one bed will fit on the others. The beds should be built east and west, and as level as possible. After the trench has been dug, set posts (gas pipe is preferable to anything else) along each side of the trench. These should be five feet apart. The row on the north side should extend one foot above the level of the ground, and the row on the south side six inches above. Planks are then placed on the inside of the rows of posts and fastened to them by means of a wire, run through the boards and around the posts, that is, if gas pipes are used; if not, the boards are nailed to the stakes. Planks from one to two inches in thickness are generally used. If the soil where the beds are built, is of a loose nature, it will be necessary to board the trench up to keep the walls from "caving in," this will also prevent rats, mice and moles from getting into the bed.

When the frame is in place and made secure, a strip of inch board, wide enough to serve as rest for the edges of two sash, and having an upright strip in the center, should be fastened across the bed where each two sashes meet.

PREPARING THE BED.

The simple principles involved in the preparation of manure for hot-beds, is to most gardeners a very mysterious subject. "Many growers fear the uncertainties connected with this method of heating beds. The yeast fungus, which is the cause of fermentation, if once introduced into a manure heap suitable to its growth, spreads quite rapidly and soon has the whole mass in a state of heat."

Fresh manure from the horse stable, mixed with half its bulk of urine soaked litter or leaves from the woods makes the best heating material. It is richer than most any other kind of manure, especially if the horses have been highly fed on grain, bran, oil meal, etc. The best substitute for horse manure is sheep droppings, or a mixture of the two will give good results.

In order to thoroughly mix and get the manure to an even temperature throughout, it should be drawn to some convenient place near the beds, and thrown in a conical pile. In a few days it will begin to heat, which will be indicated by the escape of steam from the heap, it should then be forked over and thoroughly shaken up, and the lumps torn apart. In turning, care should be taken to throw the manure that was on the outside of the pile into the center of the new heap just being formed. If in two or three days the heap is again fermenting nicely, as it should if it has received the proper treatment, it is ready to be placed in the bed.

If the manure is already very hot tread it down firmly; but if fermentation has only just begun, leave the manure loose and fill up clear to the top of frames. After fermentation has again become active it should be leveled off where needed, and tramped down solid.

The bed is now ready for the soil, which should have been previously prepared so as to put it on at once in order to be warmed by the heat coming from the manure. "Soil to be in the best condition for this purpose, should have been prepared the previous fall. * * * It must be rich and fine, and consist of about one-third well rotted compost and two-thirds good loam, rotton turf, &c."

CHAPTER XXII.

COLD FRAMES.

"COLD frames are simple affairs—box-like structures covered with sashes." The construction of cold frames is very much the same as for hot-beds, about the only difference is in the depth. No manure is used in cold frames, that is for heating purposes, therefore the excavation is only from six to ten inches deep. They should be built in the same plot with the hot-beds, running east and west, or north and south, according to conture of the land. One of the principle uses to which cold frames are put, is the wintering over of such plants as cabbage, cauliflower, etc.

THE SASH

For cold frames and hot-beds are the most expensive part in their construction. Owing to the large demand for these sash, various factories throughout the United States have provided themselves with special machinery by which they are manufactured in large quantities, and can be ordered through almost any general supply store. The average price for these sash, already glazed and painted, is something less than two dollars per sash. Some growers claim that it is cheaper to buy the sash unglazed, and put the glass in on rainy days and at odd times when work is a little scarce.

This is especially advisable if there is an empty building of any kind in which the work can be done, as the manufacturers are liable to use the cheapest grade of paint and putty they can find, and the glass is also more liable to get broken in the sash than when boxed up, in shipping. The number of sash required for market gardening, will depend entirely upon the amount, and line of work expected to be engaged in. For general market gardening, twenty-five to thirty sash per acre of ground devoted to the business, will suffice; while the gardener who expects to raise nothing but such vegetables as spinach, lettuce, radishes, carrots, beets, cucumbers, etc., will require eight or ten times this amount per acre, and a still larger number would be necessary where nothing but plants, to sell to other gardeners, are grown. Plant-raising often proves quite profitable to those that live a short distance from large cities.

EXTRA COVERING FOR FRAMES AND HOT-BEDS.

During the colder part of winter, and especially when a "cold snap" comes, the beds and frames should have some extra covering of some sort.

Shutters used for additional covering are made the same size of the sash. The material should be of some kind of light wood, not over one-half inch in thickness, white pine is preferred to anything else, as it is both light and durable. A board one-half inch thick will keep out as much cold as a board two inches or more in thickness, and are not so expensive, and are much more convenient to handle.

Mats, however, are much more effective, and where hot-beds are used, they are almost indispensable. They can be made by the most unskilled workman, and during winter weather and rainy days, when there is nothing else to do.

A supply of long rye, wheat or oat straw, should always be kept on hand, and at odd times worked up into mats. "Their manufacture is a simple thing indeed. Make a frame seven by four feet and tightly stretch four or five parallel stout tarred strings, ten or twelve inches apart, from top to bottom. Have as many balls of lighter tarred string, and fasten on to each upright string at the bottom, leaving the balls in front of the frame. Now lay a whisk of straw, cut sides out, in the junction of the strings at the bottom, and fasten it there by twisting each of the smaller strings once around the straw and the upright string. Next put on another whisk of straw, and continue until the frame is full, and the mat is finished."

Thus during the run of a year, quite a large number of these mats can be made.

The best straw for the purpose, is rye cut before the grain has formed, and the gardener that has much business about him, will grow a little patch of rye, cut and store it away at the proper time, to work up in the coming season.

MANAGEMENT.

Cold Frames.—If it be desired to winter plants over for spring planting, the cold frames should be used. In the northern states, the seed of cauliflower, cabbage and lettuce should be sown in the open ground from the 15th to the 20th of September. The seed should not be sown too early, as this will cause many of them to run to seed and of course they are then useless; again if sown too late, cold weather will set in before the plants have grown enough to stand the winter.

Within a month from time of sowing the seed, the plants will be of sufficient size to be transplanted in the frames. Eight hundred lettuce plants, or five hundred cauliflower or cabbage plants, may be set under each three by six foot sash.

These plants are almost hardy, and will stand severe freezing without injury. It is not necessary to put the sash on for a month or six weeks after transplanting, unless a severe cold spell should come for a few days, which is quite often the case. If it is necessary to thus temporarily protect the plants, care should be taken to remove the sash again, as soon as the weather will permit, so as to harden the plants for winter. During cold weather, even on clear winter days, when the temperature is down to fifteen degrees in the shade, they should be abundantly aired by tilting up the sash at the back, or, better still, when the day is mild, by taking the sash entirely off. If the plants have been thoroughly hardened, there is no use for any other covering but the sash, except during extreme cold weather, when the thermometer falls to 15° below zero. In the spring when the weather has moderated, and it is not necessary to keep the sash on the plants, the sash are placed on frames that have been covered up with straw or leaves in sufficient depth to keep the ground from freezing, so that they may be got at and be in condition to be planted in lettuce by the end of February or first of March. After the soil in the frames has been well enriched by mixing in about three inches of well rotted manure, fifty lettuce plants are set under each sash. After the plants are set they require but little attention; the only thing to attend to is to give plenty of air, and on mild, rainy days to remove the sash entirely, so that the beds may receive a thorough wetting.

A crop of lettuce thus grown will be fit for market in about six weeks from the time of transplanting. After the lettuce has been taken from the frames, which will be about the 15th of May, cucumber plants are taken from the forcing-house or hot-bed, and planted in the frames, four or five under each sash. The sash are left on until June, when the crop begins to be sold.

The cucumber, being a tropical plant, requires a warmer temperature than lettuce, and is very sensitive to cold, but on warm days airing should never be neglected, as the sun's rays would raise the temperature under the glass to such an extent as to injure, if not entirely destroy, the crop.

Hot-Beds.—Immediately after the heating material and soil have been placed in the bed, it should be covered with sash and be kept closed until the heat rises; at this time a thermometer plunged in the heating material, should indicate 100°, but this is too hot for almost any vegetable growth. Operations of sowing or planting in the hot-bed should not be commenced until the intense heat and rank steam caused by fermentation, has subsided, which it will do in about three days. Beginners often lose the first crop, owing to their impatience to get the beds planted.

Hot-beds are used for various purposes. One of the most important uses is the forcing of lettuce. The plants are taken from the cold frames and planted in the hot-bed, fifty under each sash, the first crop by second week in January. Under proper management the first crop will be ready for market by the first of March, giving plenty of time for another crop to be grown in the same bed. The bed, however, by this time is no longer a hot-bed, the manure having become exhausted, and it is treated exactly as a cold frame.

Another use to which hot-beds are put is the raising of tomato, egg and pepper plants. The seed should be sown about March 10th, with temperature the same as before described. In sowing, it is well not to cover the seed more than a quarter of an inch, with some very light mold; leaf mold and sand are very desirable, firming it gently with a board.

Close attention to airing during the hot part of the day, and covering up at night, is essential, and also that the soil be kept moist, but not soaked.

The night temperature may range from fifty five to sixty-five, and in the day time from seventy to eighty degrees.

As soon as the seedlings are about an inch high they should be taken up and transplanted into a more extensive hot-bed, for they now begin to develope and require more room. One hundred plants may be set under a sash. After transplanting they should receive a thorough watering, and also, shaded from the sun until they have struck root, which will be in two or three days.

Hot-beds are also used for growing cabbage, cauliflower and lettuce, for out door spring planting, when a supply has not been wintered over in the cold frames. The seeds are sown in February or March, according to latitude of the grower, and treated the same as tomatoes, &c., with the exception that a slightly cooler temperature be maintained.

Clear Cypress Greenhouse ⊙ Material.

We carry in stock many different designs of Rafters, Sash Bars and everything else from the bottom of gutters up. Our facilities are large, and we are prepared to furnish on short notice material of our own designs or any special designs, and all of open-air-dried clear Cypress Lumber. Every foot of our stock is guaranteed Spot Clear. Write for circulars and estimates. No trouble to furnish plans when necessary.

We build Greenhouses complete

And, having had wide experience we know all the requisites and guarantee superior construction.

Lockland Lumber Co.,

Lockland, Ohio.

E. HIPPARD,

Manufacturer and Patentee

. . . of the . . .

New Standard Ventilating Machinery and Greenhouse Appliances.

Send for Illustrated Catalogue

YOUNGSTOWN, OHIO.

"The Market Garden."

A Monthly Journal for Market Gardeners
and Vegetable Growers.

SAMPLE COPY FREE.

50c Per Year.

A Practical Paper

FOR

Practical People.

The Market Garden contains illustrated articles on every phrase of vegetable culture by practical and experienced writers. It includes many departments, such as Vegetable Diseases and their remedies, questions and answers, correspondence, new varieties and their tests, articles on greenhouse construction and their management, etc.

SEND FOR SAMPLE COPY.

THE MARKET GARDEN CO.

536 Boston Block,

MINNEAPOLIS, MINN.

www.ingramcontent.com/pod-product-compliance
Lightning Source LLC
Chambersburg PA
CBHW030314170426
43202CB00009B/998